THE PHASES OF THE MOON

By George Pendergast

Gareth Stevens
PUBLISHING

Please visit our website, www.garethstevens.com. For a free color catalog of all our high-quality books, call toll free 1-800-542-2595 or fax 1-877-542-2596.

Library of Congress Cataloging-in-Publication Data

Pendergast, George, author.
The phases of the moon / George Pendergast.
    pages cm. — (Cycles in nature)
 Includes bibliographical references and index.
ISBN 978-1-4824-1663-3 (pbk.)
ISBN 978-1-4824-1664-0 (6 pack)
ISBN 978-1-4824-1662-6 (library binding)
1. Moon—Phases—Juvenile literature. 2. Moon—Juvenile literature. I. Title.
 QB588.P46 2015
 523.3'2—dc23

                          2014032406

Published in 2016 by
Gareth Stevens Publishing
111 East 14th Street, Suite 349
New York, NY 10003

Copyright © 2016 Gareth Stevens Publishing

Designer: Sarah Liddell
Editor: Ryan Nagelhout

Photo credits: Cover, p. 1 pockygallery/Shutterstock.com; p. 5 panbazil/
Shutterstock.com; p. 7 gunarex/Shutterstock.com; p. 9 Vadim Sadovski/
Shutterstock.com; p. 11 (moon) AstroStar/Shutterstock.com; p. 11 (earth) Fisherss/
Shutterstock.com; p. 13 Nadezhda Bolotina/Shutterstock.com; p. 15 (waxing crescent)
Stefan Holm/Shutterstock.com; p. 15 (first quarter) Myotis/Shutterstock.com;
p. 17 (waxing gibbous) Claudio Divizia/Shutterstock.com; p. 17 (full) apiguide/
Shutterstock.com; p. 19 (waning gibbous) Natursports/Shutterstock.com; p. 19 (last
quarter) Procy/Shutterstock.com; p. 21 Palmer Kane LLC/Shutterstock.com.

Printed in the United States of America

CPSIA compliance information: Batch #CS16GS: For further information contact Gareth Stevens, New York, New York at 1-800-542-2595.

CONTENTS

Boldface words appear in the glossary.

Looking Up

When you look up in the sky on a clear night, you can usually see the moon. But what about nights when we can only see part of the moon? What's happening to the moon then?

Sometimes we can see a full, round moon on a clear night. Other times we can only see half of it! These are two **phases** of the moon. We see different amounts on different days.

7

We see the moon in the sky because of the sun. It shines light on the moon, which reflects, or bounces back, toward Earth. We can only see the part of the moon that's facing Earth and lit up by the sun.

9

The Eight Phases

As the moon **circles** Earth, it's always lit on one side. However, the amount of the lit side we see changes. This creates the phases of the moon. There are eight different phases of the moon. It takes 29.5 days to complete the **cycle** of phases.

The Phases of the Moon

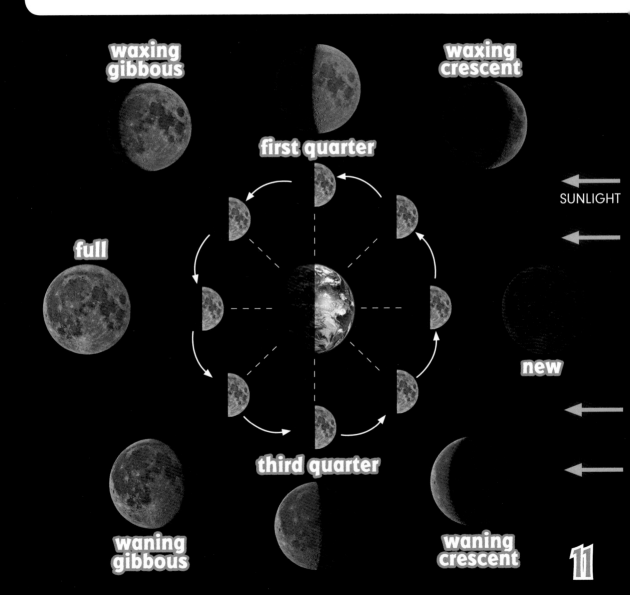

waxing gibbous

waxing crescent

first quarter

SUNLIGHT

full

new

third quarter

waning gibbous

waning crescent

11

Follow the Leader

The phases of the moon always happen in the same order. When the moon is directly between Earth and the sun, you can't see it at all. This is called a "new" moon. Only the side of the moon we can't see is lit by the sun. When there is a new moon, the night sky looks very dark.

Waxing and First Quarter

As the moon moves around Earth, we start to see part, or a **crescent**, of its right side lit by the sun. This is called a waxing crescent moon. "Waxing" means that the amount of the moon we see is growing. A few days later we see a quarter moon. It's also called a first quarter moon.

waxing crescent moon

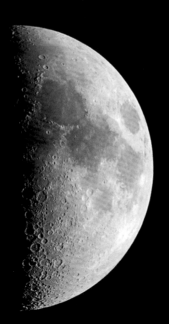

first quarter moon

15

Full Moon

As days go by, more of the moon is **visible**. When the moon is three quarters visible we call it a waxing **gibbous** moon. Soon, the moon is full! We can see its full shape on a clear night. This happens about 2 weeks after a new moon.

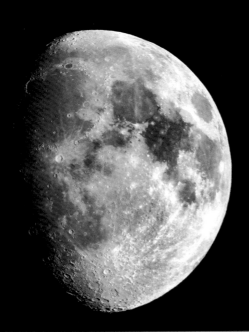

waxing gibbous moon

full moon

Waning and Third Quarter

Now the moon starts to **wane**!
In the next phase, called waning
gibbous, the right side of the
moon starts to disappear. Three
weeks after a new moon, we see
only the left half of the moon.
This is the last quarter, or third
quarter, moon.

waning gibbous moon

last quarter moon

19

Gone So Soon?

The final phase of the moon shows us only a little bit of the left side of the moon. This is called the waning crescent moon. In a few days, the moon is "new" again, and we start the cycle all over!

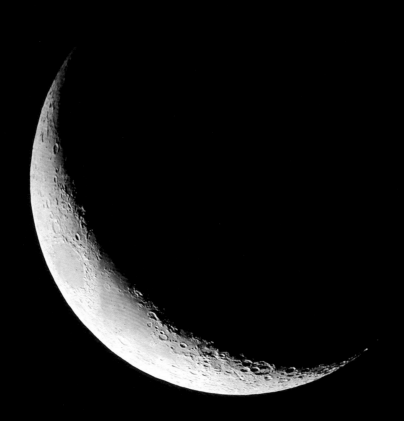

waning crescent moon

GLOSSARY

circle: to go around

crescent: a curved shape

cycle: a series of events that happen over and over again

gibbous: seen with more than half but less than a full disk lit

phase: a step in a series of events

visible: able to be seen

wane: to grow smaller in size or amount seen

FOR MORE INFORMATION

BOOKS

Owen, Ruth. *The Moon*. New York, NY: Windmill Books, 2014.

Sexton, Colleen. *The Moon*. Minneapolis, MN: Bellwether Media, 2010.

Slade, Suzanne. *The Phases of the Moon*. New York, NY: PowerKids Press, 2007.

WEBSITES

Earth's Moon
moon.nasa.gov/home.cfm
Find out more about the moon on this NASA (National Aeronautics and Space Administration) website.

Moon Phase Images
tycho.usno.navy.mil/vphase.html
See what phase of the moon is visible on a certain day and time on this site.

INDEX

How to Make Your Dog #famous

*To Chlo, the pup who started it all
and changed my life for the best.*

Loni Edwards

How to Make Your Dog #famous

A guide to social media and beyond

Laurence King Publishing

Contents

ROAD
TO
FAME

The Perfect Team

Humans and dogs have been a team for centuries. What began as a working partnership quickly evolved into an emotional one—there is archeological evidence of humans caring for a sick puppy dating back over 14,000 years. Today, dogs are our best friends: they sleep in our beds, we treat them like children, and we often prioritize their needs over our own. As we began to share our lives and human friendships through digital platforms, bringing our dogs into the mix was a natural progression. In turn, social media helped strengthen the age-old bond between humans and dogs.

Today, people can interact with dogs across the world at the touch of a screen, digitally experiencing the joy and emotions of this enduring relationship. While it's a given that dogs are universally loved, they're also media and marketing gold. They avoid scandals, bring a positive energy, and appeal to all types of people around the world. As a result, people are following dogs on social media in record numbers, and the media, marketers, and brands have taken note.

**The "dog influencer" was born,
and your pup could be the next star.**

As the founder of The Dog Agency, and the human to one of the original dog influencers, Chloe (@chloetheminifrenchie, opposite and page 131), I've been in this world since the early 2010s. My start was an accidental one. The moment Chloe came into my life I was in awe of her ability to spread joy—every time I looked at her I found myself smiling from ear to ear—so I decided to create an Instagram account to share photos and videos of her with my friends and family. Her adorable smile and photogenic personality quickly drew a large following from around the world and before I knew it I had a dog influencer on my hands. With my legal background and my first-hand pet influence experience, I decided to create The Dog Agency—the first talent management agency to focus on pet influencers, to fill the need for structure in the emerging pet influencer industry. Since then I've helped develop hundreds of pet influencers and worked with countless brands and media partners, and I'm excited to share with you the knowledge I've accumulated through the years.

In this book, you will learn how to make your dog famous in a fun and rewarding way, all while strengthening the bond between you and your pup. You'll discover that there is no single formula for success. Instead, your success will come from creating a unique brand that adds value to your community, staying true to that uniqueness throughout your journey, and, most importantly, enjoying the experience.

But before we start down the Road to Fame, it's important to understand how to be a good dog parent. Your top priority should always be to keep your pup happy and healthy. The following pages will cover how to understand their behavior so you can interpret how they are feeling, how to set your pup up for success in their day-to-day life, and the basics of health and wellness.

Now, grab your furry best friend, curl up on the couch, flip the page, and let's get started!

Learn How to Speak Dog

To understand how your pup is feeling, regularly monitor their facial expressions and body posture. The best way to do this is holistically. For example, raised fur could mean your pup is either scared or excited, so look at the bigger picture: consider their personality and check their other expressions, and you'll be better able to determine which emotion they're experiencing.

If your pup is showing signs of fear, remove them from the situation and take note of what they are reacting to. If it is safe to do so, take a video to share with a professional, like a trainer or veterinarian, who can work with you to help desensitize your pup to the stressor so it doesn't scare them in the future.

▶ Relaxed

- Head in its natural position
- Ears in their natural position
- Soft eyes with a neutral forehead
- Open or relaxed mouth with unclenched teeth, or closed mouth with no tension in lips
- Tail in its natural position
- Neutral posture
- Non-raised fur

▶ Excited or playful

- Moving head
- Perked ears
- Wide and clear eyes
- Open or relaxed mouth with unclenched teeth, or closed mouth with no tension in lips
- Raised or wagging tail
- Loose and wiggly posture, or in a play-bow position
- Raised fur

- -

▶ Nervous or fearful

- Lowered head
- Ears tucked against head
- Fully open eyes with large pupils and whites showing
- Tightly closed mouth with corners pulled back, possible drooling
- Tail tucked between legs
- Crouched posture, or trying to escape
- Raised fur

Set Your Pup Up for Success

Once you understand your dog's cues, you can help them navigate life in a positive way. From paying extra attention when your pup is in an unfamiliar situation, to letting people know how best to interact with your dog, you are now your pup's voice.

Pay Attention

You should always pay attention to your dog's behavioral cues to understand how they are feeling, but this is especially important when your dog is in an unfamiliar or unpredictable environment in which their level of comfort is unknown or could quickly change. Children, for example, tend to lack a sense of boundaries and might not know how to properly interact with a dog. This unpredictable environment could lead to an unpleasant situation for either your pup or the child if you don't pay attention.

Create Guidelines

Know what your dog likes and doesn't like—and communicate that up-front. You know your dog best, and it's important for you to be their voice. Does your dog like to be cuddled? Are they comfortable being around other dogs? Do they have any particular sensitivities? Set guidelines so people know how to best interact with your dog.

When Emma, my second Frenchie, was a puppy, she had a tendency to get nervous around unfamiliar dogs. I worked on desensitizing her by slowly introducing her to new pups, but sometimes, when we were on a walk, an unfamiliar dog would try to run up to her. To keep her from getting stressed, I'd politely let the other dog's human know that Emma gets nervous around new dogs. They would keep their dog back, and a stressful situation was avoided.

Encourage Development

Socializing your dog at a young age will help create a well-adjusted pup who feels comfortable in new situations. The critical socialization period for puppies occurs around 3 to 15 weeks of age, however, it's never too late to start training and guiding your dog to be their best self.

Introduce your pup to new people, places, dogs, smells, crowds, and other new situations in a slow and thoughtful manner, while paying attention to their behavioral cues. Remember, if they're showing signs of stress, remove them from the situation and try again another day with a less stressful situation. For example, if they're overwhelmed at the dog park, focus on making sure they're comfortable playing with one new dog before reintroducing them to the whole pack.

PRO TIP

When working on introducing your pup to new situations, bring treats to create positive associations (more on that in Road to Fame: Training 101, page 36).

11

Prioritize Health and Wellness

To prepare your pup for a healthy and happy life, exercise them, both physically and mentally, maintain a healthy weight through a nutritious and well-balanced diet, avoid toxic foods, schedule regular veterinary check-ups, and seek an expert's advice the moment you think something might be wrong.

Mental and Physical Fitness

A well-exercised mind and body are the key to a happy and well-behaved dog. Learning and practicing tricks, and playing with puzzles and interactive toys, are great forms of mental exercise. They alleviate boredom and help direct your pup's energy to positive activities.

Walks and playtime are great forms of physical exercise. The amount of exercise a pup needs depends on a variety of factors—most notably, the breed and age of the dog. Check with your veterinarian to determine how much physical activity your pup needs to ensure they're getting the right amount.

Diet

Select well-balanced and nutritious food and treats, paying attention to portion size. Treats should make up no more than 10 percent of your dog's daily caloric intake. If they've already eaten their daily allotment (and they haven't been extra active), don't give in to the puppy eyes and overfeed them. Just because they're cute and begging for food doesn't mean they're hungry and need more snacks!

Be aware that human food can be toxic to your pup. The biggies to watch out for are chocolate (the darker it is, the more toxic), grapes and raisins, and xylitol (artificial sweetener).

Wellness

Visit your vet regularly for a physical exam, vaccinations, bloodwork, heartworm test, and fecal analysis, and to check that your pup is maintaining a healthy weight. If your pup is young and healthy, go to the vet at least once a year. If your dog is older, visit the vet at least twice a year. Wellness check-ups are important, because, just as with humans, the earlier a problem is detected the better.

Be Prepared

Know where your closest, trusted emergency veterinary hospital is located, save the number of an animal poison control center in your phone, and keep a doggie first-aid kit on hand. Some good things to have in your first-aid kit include a thermometer, fresh 3 percent hydrogen peroxide, tweezers, sterile saline solution (for eye wash and rinsing wounds), antibiotic wound spray or ointment, gauze, and non-stick bandages.

If you sense something is wrong with your dog, trust your instincts and speak with a vet right away. It's better to be safe than sorry. If you can't physically get to the vet, there are great digital telehealth services available that allow you to connect with a vet via your phone or computer to get an expert opinion. Choose a service now and set up an account so you have it ready when you need it. Not everything can be handled digitally (diagnostics, for example), but telehealth is a great way to quickly connect with a vet to assess the situation.

Lastly, while you may think of your pup as a little human, always check with your vet before giving them human medications. While some, in the correct formulas and doses, are safe and can help (some antihistamines and antacids, for instance), others can be very dangerous (most painkillers).

Play Up Your Features

You know what they say: If you've got it, flaunt it! Take your dog's best feature—for example, their ears—and start to look for social-media trends that take advantage of this specific feature; there'll always be something. Or is there a famous dog from a film you could compare your pup to? You want to be known for something specific to make you more memorable. When capturing your dog's charms, you should make sure your picture quality is the best it can be, and try to keep the background plain so as not to distract your audience from what you're trying to promote. Remember that fame may not happen overnight, but with the right attitude and photography, you'll get there.

Ellée and Tom's Story

Winnie's Instagram started off as a bit of fun for friends and family to watch her grow. Little did we know that one of her videos would blow up on TikTok and be viewed worldwide, being shared by celebrities such as singer Rita Ora and influencer Sofia Jamora. From here on, it was a crazy journey of partnerships with many brands. It was Winnie's eyes that stole the hearts of her fans, who branded her the "Disney dog" and compared her to the likes of Lady, from the film *Lady and the Tramp*—and we couldn't agree more!

@WINNIE_THECOCKER
Winnie

Instagram: 481k
TikTok: 186k

Breed
Cocker Spaniel

Humans
Ellée Gudge and Tom Bowman

Favorite Dogs
@adogloverstale
@hi_im_parsnip
@presleythecocker

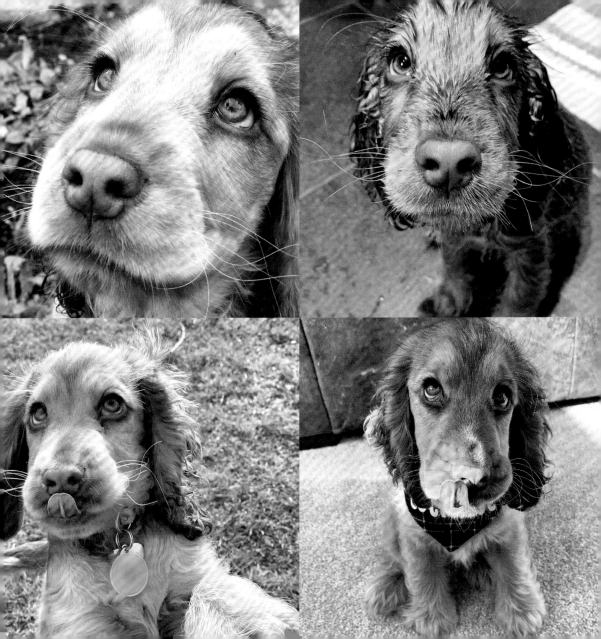

Is the Influencer Life for You?

When done right, building a successful digital presence for your dog is a fun and rewarding way to spend more quality time together and strengthen your bond, while spreading joy around the world, making new friends, and working with your favorite brands. But the influencer life is not for everyone. Step one on the Road to Fame is determining if this life is a good fit for you.

◄ Do you have a unique perspective to share?

Being original is key. What will set you apart from the crowd and cause you to stand out? Everyone thinks their pup is the best (and rightly so!), but how is your pup different? Do they have unique features like Tuna (page 20)? Maybe they do a weird thing that everyone loves? What about you? Do you have a unique perspective, creative approach, or message to share? Think about how you and your pup can be unique and add value to your community (more on this in Road to Fame: Establish Your Brand, page 24).

▲ Will you find this fun?

In addition to everything you're doing to make sure this is a positive experience for your dog, stop to think if it will be fun for you, too. Do you have a creative side you're looking to explore? Do you like creating content—coming up with creative ideas for photos and videos, setting up scenes, and writing copy? Keeping your feed active and engaging takes time and effort. Will you like building communities and engaging with people? Your new digital community will become a big part of your life—are you ready to set aside time to dive into your direct messages and comments? If this doesn't sound fun to you, you will probably fall behind with your content and fall out of touch with your community, so it might not be the right path for you.

▲ Do you have the time and energy to commit?

Building a successful digital presence for your dog requires more work than you may expect. To help find the time, make use of schedules to plan out when you're going to create and post content. Being thoughtful about how often you create content will make the process more manageable and also prevent the content from overwhelming you. If you take your dog to the beach for a fun outing, for example, grab some content at the start, and pull out your camera when they do something adorable, but between that focus on having fun and enjoying your time together.

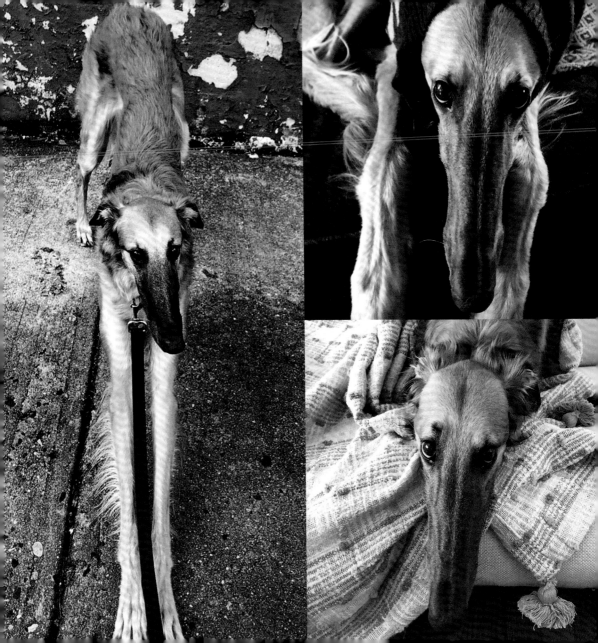

@TUPEYTHEBORZOI

Tupelo

Instagram: 80k

Breed
Borzoi

Human
Allison Cannarsa-Barr

Favorite Dogs
@mayapolarbear
@penelope_goose
@theblindborzoi

Find Your Angle

Figure out your dog's stand-out feature and play it up! Whether it's a physical trait, a funny expression, or a quirk of their personality, there is probably one part of your pup that grabs people's interest the most. Make note of how people react to your dog in real life, because this will translate to social media. Then, learn how to best accentuate this trademark trait. Doggie naps make a great opportunity for you to practice different camera distances and angles, so when the time comes to capture that perfect moment you'll know exactly what to do. Keep posting on your dog's special feature—it drives the unique and defining content that will keep viewers charmed and coming back!

Allison's Story

I was never able to have a dog until well into adulthood, so it was a big deal for me! My husband and I wanted to find one who would be a true family member, and when we discovered the borzoi breed, our lives were forever changed. With Tupe's unusual, quiet, sensitive yet goofy personality, she is without question my doggie soulmate. We understand each other so well that it makes my job as her "social-media manager" feel easy. It's her show-stopper snout that made her famous when her pictures went unexpectedly viral, but I think my genuine appreciation and understanding of her quirky personality come through on the account and make strangers around the world fall in love with her as well.

Lean Into Your Quirks

My grandmother once said to me, quoting Oscar Wilde, "Be yourself because everyone else is already taken." I took what she said very seriously. I've always tried to be unapologetically me, and once I'd embraced my quirkiness, everyone else around me seemed to as well. When I first started posting about my quirky dog, Tuna, on social media, I got mixed reviews. Some people thought he was adorable; others criticized his unconventional looks. I just continued to celebrate his differences, and, over time, his followers fell in love with his charm and his cartoonish looks. My hope is that Tuna's unique physical attributes remind you to embrace who you are, because there is no one else like you!

Courtney's Story

I had often said that I wanted to be used to change the world, but at the time, I didn't know how. I never anticipated that my unconventional pup could have such a tremendous impact on people's hearts. When I adopted Tuna, his signature teeth hadn't developed yet, but I knew there was something special about him. At the end of 2011, I created an Instagram account showcasing Tuna's unique facial expressions, and by 2013 he had gone viral in the global media. I realized then that we were changing people's days all over the world, and I'm humbled that we are catalysts for joy and laughter. While we might not be changing the world, I love being a day changer!

@TUNAMELTSMYHEART
Tuna

Instagram: 2.1m
Facebook: 379k
TikTok: 12k
Twitter: 9k
(@tuna_the_dog)

Breed
Rescue Chiweenie

Human
Courtney Dasher

Favorite Dogs
@harlowandsage
@maymothedog
@squidthegriff

@REMIXTHEDOG
Remix
Instagram: 145k

Breed
Miniature Schnauzer

Human
Chris Ha

Favorite Dogs
@crusoe_dachshund
@rustyrodas
@tofu_corgi

Craft a Signature Look

Standing out from the crowd is a must if you're looking to build a successful social-media presence. What worked well for Remix's account was when I found a signature look that allowed him to be more recognizable. Remix is known for his ability to sport glasses of any kind: whether we're on the beach or doing a photoshoot at home, there's eyewear for every occasion! It really makes for a great, versatile look that we've used to our advantage.

Chris's Story

I got Remix when he was just 8 weeks old, and he immediately became my new photography muse. I was a concert photographer for several years in Toronto, and I really enjoyed photographing Remix, as dogs and other animals provide you with a different energy and personality in front of the camera. One day, randomly, I decided to stick glasses on him, and to my surprise he was oddly comfortable with them. Eventually, *Mr Porter* magazine decided to publish what would become his most famous photo—sporting a pair of thick frame glasses with a sweater vest.

Establish Your Brand

As more and more people realize how fun, rewarding, and lucrative having a dog influencer can be, the space is getting crowded, and it requires more effort and originality to stand out. The best way to do this is to create a strong brand, with a unique perspective, to differentiate yourself. When thinking about your angle, focus on what interests and excites you.

Build your profile

The first step in establishing your brand is to build your profile. Select a handle that is easy to remember, share, and spell, and use that same handle across all your platforms (Instagram, TikTok, and so on) to stay consistent and make it easy for people to find you. Choose a profile picture that embodies your pup. Then, use the limited bio space wisely to let people know about your brand, where you're based, and how to get in contact with you. The clearer your brand comes through from your bio and content, the more likely people will be to follow you. They will better understand what your account is about, and you'll get more interest from brands (but more on that in Road to Fame: Brand Partnerships, page 96).

▲ Find your angle

How will you create compelling content to draw in an audience? Look to your dog for inspiration—what is unique or special about them? Or look inside yourself—what are you passionate about? What new perspective can you bring? Whatever you choose, make sure it's something you enjoy, so you don't lose interest. For me, it was Chlo's human-like expressions—they would always stop me in my tracks and make me smile. I've always loved taking photos, so I started snapping away. Without realizing it, we had found our angle, and we started drawing in a community of people who also found joy in her expressions.

"I'm allowed to stand in the middle of the road, because this outfit is stopping traffic."

Tika (page 30)

▲ Craft your voice

Are the captions for your images and videos going to be from your dog's perspective or yours? Do you want your content to be funny? Snarky? Inspirational? It may take a few posts to figure out what feels right for you, and what captivates your audience, but once you choose a direction, stay true to it.

The truer you stay to your voice, the more your community will feel they know you, and the stronger the connection you'll have. Additionally, it will give you a frame of reference for thinking about your account, guiding what content you create, and what partnerships make sense.

Stay consistent

Consistency is key: Stay on brand, have a consistent voice, and select a posting cadence (how often you will post new content). When thinking about posting cadence, consider what works for your schedule. For example, do you have time to create and post multiple pieces of content a week, or does posting once a week feel more reasonable? Also consider your audience. The goal is to stay relevant without inundating them with content. Keep them wanting more.

Humanize Your Dog

@Popeyethefoodie was always meant to be fun: A dog goes around town visiting pet-friendly restaurants and posing with (human) food. Initially, we looked for the best-tasting, most Instagram-worthy, or trendiest foods. Then we realized that we could often pair Popeye's humanlike expressions with the food: an excited face with a large pizza, or an activated charcoal waffle with a skeptical expression. People really related to these posts. As his following grew, we tried keeping it interesting by giving him clothes and accessories, and traveling to other cities and states. Popeye went from a stray, homeless dog to a dapper little gourmand. It's important to focus on what's easy and feels natural for your pet. Popeye's account came about because he loved to dine out with us and just happened to be really well-behaved around food.

Ivy's Story

When I found Popeye, I was working full-time for a software company and was also part of a family-owned restaurant. My restaurant responsibilities included photography and managing the social media, which was a new world for me. n getting to know Popeye, I learned he was really good at posing for photos. I wanted to make him his own Instagram account, but I wanted it to be a little bit special. When I realized how well-behaved he is around food, I coupled two of my favorite things—Popeye and food—to create the page.

@POPEYETHEFOODIE
Popeye

Instagram: 410k
Facebook: 29k

Breed
Rescue Mixed Breed

Humans
Ivy Diep

Favorite Dogs
@157ofgemma
@lokistagram
@wolfgang2242

@HI.THIS.IS.TATUM

Tatum

TikTok: 2.2m
Instagram: 311k
Facebook: 18k
YouTube: 12k (Tatum Talks)

Breed
Rescue Pit Bull

Human
Charles Lever

Favorite Dogs
@bully.baloo
@minidoodlebentley
@tedbear_super_staff

Find Your Voice

Social media has room for everyone, and everyone has their own voice. Your voice can be anything, as long as it sets you apart. Each of us has something different to offer. Finding your voice is important because you can use it to let others know how to find you in a crowd; your voice is your brand. Nobody knows you better than you know yourself, so don't force it but, once you find your voice, own it and stay loyal. People want to be offered something that nobody else can give them. Any chef can cook, but celebrity chefs entertain! The most important thing to remember is that, if you go off brand and stray from your passion, people will notice.

Charles's Story

Tatum was rescued on the very day that was supposed to be his last. After suffering severe abuse, all he wanted to do was show love and appreciation for each new day. Once I realized he had a voice, family and friends started requesting personalized videos from him. I started the Instagram account to expand on that and make it easier to keep the videos in one place. Tatum's voice, alongside his ability to jump straight up and down when he is excited, is what invited the world on this journey with us. I've developed his brand over the past year by making sure that when people see nuggets, watermelon, bow ties, or Dunkin' Donuts they think of Tatum. Showing what a rescue can become is our mission, but we had no idea the extent to which he would touch hearts.

Dress Up

Weighing in at a mere 8lbs (3.6kg), Tika is a skinny legend who combines her love for fashion with comfort. Italian greyhounds (affectionately known as iggys) are always chilly. In Montreal, the temperature varies vastly throughout the year, meaning Tika needs outfits for every season. From windbreakers to faux-fur coats, to turtlenecks, knitted snoods, and high-knee boots, everything she wears is practical, but always fabulous. With their long legs and neck, tiny waists, and large ribcages, iggys need clothing by designers specializing in the breed. Tika has worked with some very creative designers in the dog-wear industry—including Hound Around, BonGoof, LOKO Pet Apparel, and Iggy-clothing—which has provided some iconic fashion moments.

Thomas's Story

When I started Tika's account, she had one generic red sweater and a basic black collar. As her online following grew, I needed to up her fashion game to keep her photos fresh and fun. When her first package of iggy clothing arrived, we posted those outfits online and her following skyrocketed: she was a hit! She has been featured in *Vogue* and *Vogue Italia*, her posts shared by, among others, *Cosmopolitan*, *Paper*, *The Cut*, and *Elle* magazines, and her 2020 "Love It, Couldn't Wear It" TikTok video has become a viral sensation, with Justin Bieber, Jennifer Aniston, Sofía Vergara, and Oprah hitting the share button. The most important thing to remember when it comes to dog fashion is your dog's comfort. If the garment is light in weight and keeps Tika warm, then we can focus on the fun stuff, like sequins, faux fur, and pompoms.

@TIKATHEIGGY
Tika

TikTok: 1.1m
Instagram: 1m
Facebook: 25k

Breed
Italian Greyhound

Human
Thomas Shapiro

Favorite Dogs
@honeytheiggy
@penelope_goose
@squidthegriff

@COOKIEMALIBU
Cookie Dough
and Malibu

Instagram: 115k

Breed
Pomeranian

Human
Jennifer Evers

Favorite Dogs
@mayapolarbear
@tikatheiggy
@tuckerbudzyn

Add Another Pet

When adding a pet to your family, patience is always essential, especially when other furry family members are involved. You must be in control of the situation. The first meeting should preferably be in a neutral space, where there aren't any territorial tensions. Give your new pet time to adjust, while letting everyone get to know each other. If you are adding another species (we have a cat and three hedgehogs in addition to two dogs), find out in advance whether they're likely to get along. Once they're all friends, having several pets can help grow your audience, as there is nothing cuter than animals caring and showing affection for other animals. *But*, before adding any other pet, please make sure that you can cover any expenses that may occur over the years, and that you have enough space to meet your pets' needs.

Jennifer's Story

Since I was little, I always wanted to be surrounded by dogs. So, no surprise, my husband and I added Cookie Dough and Malibu to our family as soon as we could. We had no intention of creating an Instagram at all, but destiny hit us: Malibu became seriously ill and was suddenly fighting for his life. We decided to create an account for our pets, to collect all the precious moments. In a Christmas miracle, Malibu magically pulled through. Now, he smothers every new family member with love and is especially obsessed with our hedgehogs, little angels Willi Vanilli, Ed, and Liam.

Embrace the Meme

Internet memes are relatable, funny, and put into words the way we feel. Throw in an adorable pup and you have a recipe for success! Take an everyday situation and relate it to what's happening in the photo or video. Make sure the photo or video fits the message or the meme just won't work, no matter how adorable the image is. One of our favorite memes is a video of Murphy staring awkwardly into the distance while her eyes get bigger and bigger. The text reads, "When there's a 99% chance your card will decline but you swipe it anyway." It was a viral success. The meme enables you to laugh at an awkward and embarrassing situation.

Macie and Mindy's Story

We are sisters who do everything together, and running the @thatgoldendoodle social-media accounts is no exception. It's a family affair. When creating content, we try to focus on things our audience will relate to and want to share. Murphy's eyes and facial expressions are eerily human, so creating memes with her doing human things—like dieting, drinking wine, and preferring to stay home on a Friday night—works because the pictures look natural and are so relatable. Our most successful meme is a video of Murphy dressed as a stuffed teddy bear that reads, "When your landlord says 'No dogs allowed.'" It works because we all love our animals and can't imagine life without them.

@THATGOLDENDOODLE
Murphy and Malibu

Facebook: 207k
Instagram: 148k
TikTok: 104k

Breed
Goldendoodle

Humans
Macie and Mindy

Favorite Dogs
@mr.biggie
@popeyethefoodie
@reagandoodle

When there's a 99% chance your card will decline but you swipe it anyway

When your landlord says "No dogs allowed"

Everyone goes out on Friday and I'm just home like

Me on Labor Day + the day after

Training 101

Having a pup who can stay focused and calm around all sorts of stimuli, and can stay, sit, and pose on command, is a huge asset. This section covers the basics of training so you can prep your pup to be ready for content creation.

▶ Find your dog's motivator

To be successful with training you need to figure out how to motivate your pup. Motivation can take various forms, including toys and praise, but the most common is treats. When I started training my pup Emma, I tested out healthy, low-calorie treats to find the ideal one—one that motivated her, while also providing health benefits. The answer was blueberries. She loves the taste, and I love that they're full of nutrients. To maintain variety, we alternate with seedless watermelon, baked sweet potatoes, and chewable ice. Once you determine what motivates your dog, use it to reward them for good behavior so they develop positive associations with that behavior. When your dog is exhibiting behavior you want to discourage, ignore them—walk away or turn your back to them, so they develop negative associations (the loss of your attention) with that behavior.

PRO TIP

When training your pup, break up reward treats into smaller pieces, so you can go through more repetitions without feeding your pup too many treats.

Timing, consistency, and the importance of clear signals

Be thoughtful about when, and how often, you train your pup. If they are treat-motivated, train before mealtime, as opposed to after when they're full and the treat might not be as appealing. If your pup is full of energy, wait until they've used up some of their energy—on a walk, for example—and then try to train them when they're more calm and better able to focus. Timing is also important when rewarding your pup, to ensure you're giving them clear signals: reward them right away so they associate the behavior with the reward. Timing also plays a role when training your pup *not* to do something: if your pup begs for food while you're eating dinner and you give in and share a bite with them mid-meal, they'll think they're being rewarded for begging. If, instead, you wait until you've finished eating to give them a bite, they'll learn to wait patiently for you to finish eating to get their reward. Stay consistent with training sessions and commands. Sessions should be frequent and kept short. If your pup seems to be losing interest, end the session and try again later, or another day. Small doses and repetition are key. Once you've mastered a behavior at home, test it out in different settings to expand their skill set and prepare them for new situations.

Troubleshooting

If you're having trouble training with your pup, look at things from their perspective to figure out what might be confusing or overwhelming them. Perhaps there is a competing motivator, such as another dog in the area that is distracting them. And, lastly, don't be afraid to ask for help: Bring in an expert eye to catch things you may have missed.

@BRUSSELS.SPROUT

Sprout

Instagram: 177k
TikTok: 17k
(@brussels.sproutie)

Breed
Brussels Griffon

Human
Sigrid Neilson

Favorite Dogs
@kelly_bove
@owenthegriff
@rileybeann

Train and Practice

Put down the camera and actually spend some time training and practicing with your dog. By teaching him to pose, and, more importantly, hold that pose, you'll keep photoshoots stress-free and fun for you both. Start practicing a regular "sit—stay"; once your dog can reliably hold a pose for 30 seconds, up the ante by having him stay while you move around, flash a camera, etc. If you plan to use outfits or props, do a dress rehearsal and make sure your pup is comfortable. And always reward your pup with lots of treats, or playtime, during and after a shoot. Your dog is working when he's on set and posing, and he deserves to be paid for a job well done.

Sigrid's Story

I was a total "teacher's pet" growing up, so it was no surprise when I enrolled Sprout in puppy school at just 14 weeks old. I wasn't thinking about making him famous, I just wanted him to be well-behaved and well-adjusted. Pretty quickly, I realized not only how smart Sprout was, but also how much he enjoyed learning and how it really helped us bond. Training became a shared language we learned to speak, and it was easily translatable to a photo or video shoot. Recently, he was cast as a DJ in a campaign video, and I was so proud when he nailed tapping a mini turntable on cue while sporting a tracksuit and aviators—not because he was a tiny professional, but because I could tell he was confident and happy being on set.

Showcase Your Talents

If you find something your dog enjoys doing and seems to excel at, keep it fun and don't force them to do anything they don't want to. They are just like humans—they get tired and sometimes just have bad days. Take it slowly and never try anything dangerous just because you're trying to get better content. Bring along some treats to reward your dog and let them know they are doing a great job. Don't forget to record every moment, as you never know when and how your dog will surprise you.

Josephine's Story

Jojo and I were attacked by two large dogs while walking around in our apartment complex. It was a very traumatic event, and the vet was unsure whether Jojo would make it. After Jojo recovered from surgery we needed to find a way to get him physically strong again. He had put on quite a bit of weight post-surgery, so we thought water therapy would be the best option. As a break from all the recovery exercises, we decided to put Jojo on a surfboard and he instantly fell in love. He was so happy on the board and begged to surf, again and again. We entered him in some surf competitions for fun and he ended up winning a few. Jojo even got to surf with Bill Farmer, the voice of Disney's Goofy and Pluto, in the documentary series *It's a Dog's Life*.

@SUPERCORGI_JOJO
Jojo

Instagram: 119k
TikTok: 11k

Breed
Pembroke Welsh Corgi

Human
Josephine Zosa

Favorite Dogs
@itsdougthepug
@kilokilopower
@reagandoodle

@KELLY_BOVE

Envy, Zain, and Trek

TikTok: 4.7m
Instagram: 454k
Facebook: 11k
(@EnvyAndZain)

Breed
Rescue Border Collie

Human
Kelly Bove

Favorite Dogs
@bordernerd
@lizzie.bear
@reagandoodle

Get in Sync

Getting multiple dogs to stay still for a photo, especially in a specific pose, requires time, patience, and lots of training. Before asking Envy, Zain, and Trek to pose in a photo together, I spend time with each of them individually. They each have their own training sessions in which we take photos, play, and work on tricks. Teaching them a solid "stay" command was a top priority; without that it would be impossible to get a shot of all three. I spend a few minutes getting them set up for a photo while rewarding them for staying as asked. We always keep things short and fun, and the pups all love photo time!

Kelly's Story

I grew up with dogs and have always loved training. While in college, I fostered dogs for a local rescue center before adopting Envy—I couldn't resist those adorable eyes! Envy and I spent a lot of time practicing tricks and agility, and traveled around the East Coast of the USA competing. Four years later, Zain arrived, adopted at 15 months old from a Border collie rescue center in New York. He and Envy hit it off instantly and I started documenting their friendship through photos and videos that people from all over the world loved and followed through our Instagram account. Trek joined the family as an 8-week-old puppy, adopted from the same rescue center as Zain. He keeps things interesting, always making us laugh with his crazy antics. Life with Envy, Zain, and Trek is nothing short of an adventure and we wouldn't change it for the world.

Create Compelling Content

Now that you've established your brand and prepped your pup, it's time to start creating content. The more shareable your content—content that people will rush to share with their friends—the more successful you will be.

Have a plan, but go with the flow

Come in with a vision but be open to working with what you get. Flexibility and creativity are key here, as is capturing a lot of content—the more you have to work with the better. Test out different angles and perspectives: get down on your dog's level and try close-ups, for example, to have a variety of options to select from. Utilize squeaky toys and noises to get your pup's attention and capture different expressions, like head tilts. Holding toys or treats behind the camera can also help direct their attention to where you want it. Remember to reward them for good behavior after you get the shot! The majority of the content I create with Emma comes from capturing her expressions in the moment, rather than from a planned shoot. However, when we do set up a shoot, I usually hold one of her favorite treats behind the camera to direct her attention where I want it, and then make weird noises or say things like "Do you want a treat?!" in an excited voice to bring out different expressions. While it might get us some weird looks when we do it in public, it works—and Emma loves the attention and treats that come along with it!

▲ Outfits and props

Outfits and props can enhance your content, but they aren't necessary. Some pups love getting dressed up. Emma, for example, gets cold easily, so she loves wearing clothes. For her, clothes are fashion as well as function. If you're not sure how your pup feels about it, start small and create positive associations by rewarding your pup with praise and treats when they interact with the outfits/props. Once they're comfortable with them (pay attention to their behavioral cues) you can start integrating them into the content. But if they don't like it, don't force it.

▲ Aesthetic composition

Your backdrop can strengthen your content or detract from it, so be purposeful about what you include in your shots. Choose backdrops that contrast with your pup's fur, so your dog "pops"; that add a unique element, like beautiful scenery; or that are neutral, so all attention is focused on your pup. Try to avoid backdrops that detract from your content: messy homes (unless that is part of your brand) or backgrounds that blend in with the fur so your pup gets lost in the shot (unless that is an artistic angle you're going for). As always, your top priority should be your dog's comfort. If they're posing on a chair, make sure it's not wobbly; if they're posing next to other dogs, make sure they feel safe. And remember to test the lighting. Lighting can make or break a shot. At the start of the shoot, take one shot and check it for lighting, as well as for backdrop and framing, and make adjustments as needed. It's incredibly frustrating to do an entire shoot only to realize later that the lighting was too dark and the framing cut off your dog's ears.

PRO TIP

The best posts capture an expression (for example, a head tilt or smile), the eyes are in focus, and the pup's full face (including ears) is in frame. They are well lit and there is good contrast between the pup and the background.

Stay organized

Creating a lot of content is useful, but if you can't find it when you need it, it's not so helpful. Save and organize your content so you can easily locate it. Clips that you were unable to use this time could come in handy for your next project or idea, but only if you know where they are! And make sure to back up your work, whether in the cloud or on an external hard drive. Protect your hard work.

▲ Editing: photos

Unless your brand is tied to Photoshopping, don't overedit. Find the sweet spot between raw and over-produced, and use the photo-editing process as a way to clean up your shot rather than materially alter it. If you have a specific aesthetic or color palette like Ducky (page 105), adjust the image to match it. Otherwise, just consider the editing process a way to improve the quality of the photo and make your pup "pop."

COVER IMAGE

→

▲ Editing: videos

Editing videos is generally more involved than editing photos. Start by sorting through your video files, choosing the ones that fit your story best, and selecting clips from each, and then combine them in a way that tells a compelling story. When structuring your video, start with an opening hook that prominently features your pup to grab the viewer's attention. Similarly, when you post, choose a cover image that includes your pup. If you're planning to include music, make sure you have the rights to use it.

Caption Your Videos

Captioning videos humanizes your pet by expressing their feelings and thoughts. Choose a clear font (type, color, and size) and keep each caption fairly short. I recommend not using too many captions, as it becomes exhausting to read *and* watch the video. Think about your pet's personality: are they calm and friendly, or energetic and sassy? Try to reflect that in your captions. A few years ago, I discovered "DoggoLingo" from the meme community. These words are very funny, and the "broken" English fits Maya perfectly. If it's challenging to find the right caption for specific scenes, I take a break from editing, clear my mind, and try again later.

Lingli's Story

I started posting puppy pictures and videos of Maya on my personal Instagram account just to show my friends. Soon, all the content was Maya so I decided to make it her own account, @mayapolarbear, because she looked like a polar bear as a puppy. In the beginning, we didn't have many followers. After a while, I posted more videos and many of them were shared by other big pages. The account grew rapidly and we added accounts on YouTube, Facebook, and TikTok. When I don't have any content ideas, I check out videos from other pets on Instagram or YouTube to see if there are any trends or new challenges we can try out.

@MAYAPOLARBEAR
Maya

TikTok: 4.4m
Instagram: 2.1m
YouTube: 1.8m
Facebook: 997k
Twitter: 199k

Breed
Samoyed

Human
Lingli Ye

Favorite Dogs
@lecorgi
@milperthusky
@topithecorgi

@AMAZINGGRACIEDOODLE
Gracie
Instagram: 205k

Breed
Goldendoodle

Human
Fanny Karpman

Favorite Dogs
@eggnogthebulldog
@norbertthedog
@reagandoodle

Embrace Color

You don't have to go to the mountains to have a great day with your dog. We live in the center of Los Angeles and I love wandering around the city looking for bright colors and patterns—an old sign, a cool staircase, street art, gardens, anything is fair game. The one thing to keep in mind is lighting: I often drive by at different times to see where the shadows fall on the side of a building, or, when I find a cool wall painting, I make sure there is no glare coming off it. I thrive on bright colors and repeating patterns, but I want Gracie to be the highlight of my photos. Most street art doesn't come down to the ground, so I trained Gracie to stand confidently on a stool. I will admit, sometimes I take 500 shots of the same scene to get it just right!

Fanny's Story

A few years ago, I was dealing with extreme depression, so we got a dog, and, just like that, my life changed—it's much harder to be sad around a silly puppy. But it didn't happen overnight: the key was Instagram. Depression is like solitary confinement, but I started making connections on Instagram through Gracie. Soon, those connections became "real life" friendships. I was drawn to the colorful street art in Los Angeles—the bright colors make me happy! When I was out there exploring with Gracie, I was free from depression. For me, my account has always been about feeling good, finding beauty, making friends, and embracing color.

Enjoy the Cuddles

Daily adventures plus lots of exercise not only equals happy pets, it also results in many cuddles! When our dachshunds are tired, we know to whip out a camera and start capturing the moments when they settle down with Harlow, the Weimaraner. Light is your best friend when photographing your best friends! Because pets are completely unpredictable, an external flash can be key to capturing sharp images. When using natural light, watch how the light fills the space that you are shooting in throughout the day, and time your photos appropriately. A relaxed and comfortable pet is by far the easiest to photograph. Plenty of playtime, activity, and rewards beforehand can make a world of difference to your pet's behavior and mood, and the resulting photos will be adorable and the video footage priceless.

Brittni's Story

Cuddling has been a daily occurrence in our home since Harlow joined the family, in 2008. I knew right away that Harlow and our miniature dachshund, Sage, were going to have a unique bond when I saw baby Harlow snuggle up to her big (little) sister. Documenting their daily cuddles became extra special five years later when we knew that our senior pup, Sage, didn't have a lot of time left with us. Little did we know then that every dog (and cat) that entered our lives after Sage passed away would also develop that same sweet bond with Harlow, and each one would (almost literally) become attached to her.

@HARLOWANDSAGE
Harlow, Indiana, Reese, and Ezra

Instagram: 1.7m
Facebook: 522k
Twitter: 10k

Breeds
Dachshund, Weimaraner

Human
Brittni Vega

Favorite Dogs
@crusoe_dachshund
@kelly_bove
@wolfgang2242

@REAGANDOODLE
Reagan
Instagram: 503k
Facebook: 63k

Breed
Labradoodle

Human
Sandi Swiridoff

Favorite Dogs
@amazinggraciedoodle
@crusoe_dachshund
@thatgoldendoodle

Make Photoshop Magic

If you want to create scroll-stopping images, take a little time to edit your photos before posting. Like humans, my pics rarely go out in public without getting dressed up first. Experiment with editing apps like Photoshop. It may seem intimidating at first, but you know what they say: Practice makes perfect. Once you've mastered the basics, like lighting and cropping, you can kick it up a notch and have some fun. Every once in a while, I like to make some magic by combining three or more photos to make one smile-worthy image.

Sandi's Story

Reagan and I are a match made in heaven: I love taking and editing photos, and he loves to pose. He's been in front of my lens since he was a tiny pup. He loves the camera, as he quickly learned to associate it with praise and treats. I keep photo sessions short and sweet, which sets him up for success. Reagan looks so human when wearing a shirt, I can't resist photographing him doing human things, like holding a latte. Photos of Reagan and my then fostered, now adopted, grandson interacting while dressed alike captured hearts globally and brought awareness to the needs of children in foster care. I strive to add joy and positivity to people's lives. Consistently posting high-quality, lighthearted, polished, and sometimes magical images helps me do just that.

Get Up Close and Personal

Sometimes, the best shots of your pet are natural, candid ones. From day one, Barkley had unique facial expressions—he made it easy for us to capture up-close shots in which you can instantly sense what he's thinking. Most of these photos are of him just being himself. It doesn't take much setup or staging, which some pets can be uncomfortable with. Our best tips are to have great lighting and to angle the camera in a way that best displays the expression. A big smile calls for a full-front shot, whereas wide-eyed, drooly expressions need a side angle. You know your pet best! They can get so used to it, they won't even know that you just completed a full-on photoshoot while they snored on the couch.

Paul and Melissa's Story

We started Sir Charles Barkley's Instagram in May 2012, when he was born. Instagram didn't have a lot of dog accounts then, and we thought it would be fun to start one for our cute new puppy. We were fortunate that his breeder let us visit him weekly, so we were able to watch him grow even before taking him home (as were his followers). We're not sure what drew his following—a mixture of his name and his funny facial expressions? Whatever the reason, we never thought he would have so many followers. Barkley loves the attention and we think he was born knowing he's a little superstar. But the best part of all this is the friends we've met along the way.

@BARKLEYSIRCHARLES
Sir Charles Barkley

Instagram: 439k
Facebook: 39k (@barkleySC)

Breed
French Bulldog

Humans
Paul and Melissa Canda

Favorite Dogs
@bobabear
@dailywalter
@manny_the_frenchie

Build a Community

Now that you've established a brand and learned how to create compelling content, it's time to build a community that cares about what you have to say. This will be an ongoing process of both growing and nurturing your audience, online and offline.

◄ Be genuine, relatable, and add value

Build solid connections by sharing personal stories and keeping it real. The more you let your community in, the more connected they will feel to you and the stronger the bond you'll have. Another upside to being genuine and authentic is that it will make running your account easier and more enjoyable because you'll be posting what comes naturally to you. Lastly, the more your community relates to your content, the more likely they'll be to share it with their friends, leading to further growth of your community.

Give people a reason to follow you by adding value to their lives. This can take many forms, from providing information to spreading joy. The more value your audience gets from following you, the more likely they'll stick around.

Get discovered

Not all growth comes from a viral moment or a press feature. Maximize organic growth by using hashtags to find accounts with similar content, and engage with them. If you have a Frenchie, for example, go through the #frenchie and #frenchbulldog hashtags, and like and comment. Don't just leave an emoji as a comment—truly engage and build relationships. This will increase your visibility to the accounts you're interacting with as well as to their audience. Use hashtags on your content but don't go overboard: stick to a handful of relevant hashtags so you are discovered by the right audiences without coming across as spammy. Adding locations to your posts and tagging brands that appear in your content (or using their hashtags) are also great ways to get discovered. The brand might even ask to repost you, which could lead to further discovery. These strategies will result in you being seen by more and more people. If you're creating content that interests them, they'll be inclined to tap the follow button and stick around, and your community will grow.

▲ Respond to comments and messages

After you post, stay online and respond to all your comments and messages. Ask questions to keep the conversation going. If you have the bandwidth, also engage with the people who liked your post but didn't comment. While all this takes time, it goes a long way in strengthening your bond with your community. It shows them that you care about them and value what they have to say. They will be excited to hear from you and it will incentivize them to engage with you more.

▲ Collaborate

Having other influencers in your content adds an extra element, mixing it up and keeping your content fresh. Collaboration also comes with the added bonus of leveraging each other's networks to further your process of getting discovered and growing your community. Personally, getting to know other influencers and collaborating with them has resulted in some of my closest friendships.

▲ Get offline

Go to events, like PetCon, where you can meet and network with other influencers and fans. This will allow you to build deeper connections by bringing your online relationships offline, while also expanding your network. And when you get recognized at these events, take the time to truly connect with your fans in real life and strengthen the relationship. Having stickers of your pup on-hand to give to your fans is always a sweet touch!

PRO TIP

Once you've developed relationships with other influencers, start collaborating with them. Collaboration comes with so many benefits. Working with others is fun, you'll learn from one another, and you'll have someone else to brainstorm and get creative with.

Show Everyday Life

There can be pressure to make all social-media content perfect, but something that has allowed us to connect with our audience is our authenticity. Most of our content is simple: Bronson cuddling, playing, making funny noises—just doing regular dog things! I try to focus on sharing him and his personality, and don't sweat the small things, like filters and a beautifully curated feed. Encourage your dog to be themselves by rewarding them with treats and praise when they do something cute or funny, to reinforce that behavior. Capture as much as you can when you are having a good moment, so you have several pieces to upload later if you or your dog don't feel up to filming new content. People enjoy seeing a well-loved and cared-for pet, even if they're not doing something extraordinary.

Sydnee's Story

I created an Instagram page for Bronson so I wouldn't spam my friends on my personal page. Within a year, we went from 100 followers to over 200k. Bronson's page blew up after a video of him going down the stairs went viral, and that's when we realized we had a dog who was pretty funny just as he was. I knew that I had to find a way for the account to mesh naturally with our day-to-day life. I had to find a way to make it fun for me so that I would be motivated to engage with his audience. Luckily, Bronson made that easy, and we were able to continue to grow his page just by sharing him being himself, at home and out and about in our daily lives.

@_BRONSONTHEBULLY
Bronson
Instagram: 249k

Breed
American Bully

Human
Sydnee Gilletti

Favorite Dogs
@clydethebully_
@oso_n_koa
@what_about_bunny

@MR.BIGGIE
Mr. Biggie

TikTok: 134k
(@mr.biggiebear)
Instagram: 114k
Facebook: 11k
(@mr.biggie2016)

Breed
Pug

Humans
Sabrina Lopez and Leo
Anguiano

Favorite Dogs
@157ofgemma
@_darlin_clementine
@michanipug

Interact with Your Community

If you don't want a bunch of ghost followers, show your followers the same love that they show you. Make somebody's day by liking and responding to their comments. Use Instagram polls to invite your followers to help you make those tough life decisions, like "What shirt should Mr. Biggie wear to lunch: plaid or stripes?" Give your followers the opportunity to know you better by letting them ask you questions; pick your favorites and reply to those. And engage with other accounts. Like and comment on posts you really enjoy, and don't be afraid to share other people's awesome content (make sure to tag them when you do). Put these simple tips into action to grow your account and build a lively community.

Sabrina and Leo's Story

We were instantly obsessed when Biggie came into our lives! We wanted to document everything he did, from his first high-five to the first shirt he put on. Our personal Instagram pages became flooded with pictures and videos of him, so we decided he should have his own page. We had no idea there was a huge community of pet parents with social-media pages for their fur babies. It was cool to see that we weren't the only ones crazy enough to make a page for their dog. It didn't take long for other people to fall in love with his big personality and charming googly eyes. We're so grateful for the happiness he's brought us. And thanks to social media, he can bring happiness to many other people all over the world!

Be Relatable

You don't need to be fancy or extravagant to achieve an engaged audience. People like to see what is familiar to them. If you're lucky enough to create something to which people can relate an existing memory, that can generate very powerful emotion. When you make someone cry or laugh, that person is not just one more follower, but an engaged audience member who will genuinely love your content because it connects to something they genuinely love in real life. Our content is always very down-to-earth and unedited. In our videos and photos, and even the comics, no one is made up—we display our flaws and the house is often a mess. But at the core of all this mess are real love and humor, which people can relate to because no one is perfect, and, hopefully, we can all laugh about our shortcomings.

Gemma's Story

I've always used comics as a way of journaling. I was working at a prestigious architecture studio when I began drawing comics about my life on my subway commutes. These personal vignettes quickly became centered on my pug Mochi, because that's who I missed most during my long work hours. I started publishing my comics about Mochi on my Instagram account. They immediately took off and gained a very engaged and loyal audience. Who knew that what I thought was so personal and unique about Mochi would strike such a chord and be so incredibly relatable to a worldwide audience?

@157OFGEMMA
Mochi

Instagram: 344k
Facebook: 167k

Breed
Pug

Human
Gemma Gené

Favorite Dogs
@mr.biggie
@pugridesshotgun
@thelilgremlins

Just trying to see how many dogs I could fit on one dog bed.
My version of a clown car.
#andacat

Doesn't it look like he's telling a ghost story while holding a flashlight under his chin?
"... and then the young couple in the stalled car on the deserted highway late at night, heard a slight noise on the roof. Scrape, scrape, scrape ..., like the sound of a hook!"

I wish we saw the world as dogs do, without judgment of their color or where they come from. But unfortunately, that's not true and it's time to dig deep and find a way to make that happen.

I have kind of a weird obsession with creepy pictures. Pictures that at first glance appear to be benign, but upon closer inspection have something disturbing in the background. Like this seemingly sweet picture of Fernando after breakfast. But if you look closely ...
#ghostofbreakfastpast

@WOLFGANG2242
Edna, Melvin, and Edsel
Instagram: 1m

Breeds
Rescue Mixed Breed

Human
Steve Greig

Favorite Dogs
@harlowandsage
@lifeofpikelet
@popeyethefoodie

Go into Detail

No one knows their pets better than their owner. Your posts should describe your pet as you see them. People often write posts that are too short, from which you don't learn about their pet's personality. And then there are people who write so much that their followers lose interest. The goal is to relay the pet's personality as it relates to the picture you've taken. This allows people, little by little, to get to know that pet, and they start getting attached because they know how the pet reacts to different situations. I will write a caption about the members of my menagerie (the many senior rescue dogs, Bikini the pig, Betty the chicken, and Tofu the turkey) and wait to post—I'll take half a day and reread it and change it several times to make sure it sounds the way I talk. I want each post to read as though I am having a conversation with a friend.

Steve's Story

I'm the last person in the world that you'd expect to have a million followers. I'm not a photographer and I know only the bare basics about technology. I'm not interested in staying on top of the next tech thing, but most of the audience isn't either. I noticed, at parties, how people would talk about their dogs. They were succinct and interesting, and it drew me in—so that is how I approach my captions. Your audience wants a post they can relate to. My posts are honest and real, and I think that's what makes them popular.

Get Press

Press can give your account a boost by introducing you to new audiences, while helping build your offline presence and credibility. Here is how to be newsworthy.

BuzzFeed staff writer, Syd Robinson

Instagram: @pug_milf
Twitter: @sydrobinson_

What catches your eye and how do you choose which pups to feature?

"A lot of it is based on numbers, so basically just what goes viral. You usually get a feeling when something is going to blow up. Personally, I love content that shows a pet's unique quirks and habits. That always gets my attention!"

What advice do you have for pups looking to get discovered?

"Some things that I've learned are important are posting quality content, over quantity, playing up your pet's personality, and actively interacting with other accounts on social media."

What should pup owners *not* do?

"Don't post poor-quality—like too dark or too pixelated—pictures and/or videos of your pet!"

Good Morning America associate producer, Sara Russell

Instagram: @sararussell22
Twitter: @sararussell22

What catches your eye and how do you choose which pups to book?

"All media outlets are different when looking for animal stories, but for GMA there has to be a human-interest story involved. What is it that is making the pet and human owner together special? For example, we featured a therapy dog who serves the firefighters in California [@kerith_the_golden_retriever – see above]—human interest, plus a nice tie to current events and news headlines at the time. We also like to see a high number of followers or at least one viral video or photo.

What advice do you have for pups looking to get discovered?

"My best advice is to start with a small local following. Go to local outdoor events, connect with your community, tag the events online, and start to connect with people in person when it's safe to do so. All pet stories are also about their owners. What makes your dog/owner story different? Do you volunteer at local events? Are you donating sales from your puppy merchandise to local and national causes? What is the news headline going to be?

Keep up with social-media trends, memes, and pop culture: finding a creative way to get your pup involved will draw in more clicks and views. There are so many professional Instagram dog accounts, so how is your content going to stand out?"

What should pup owners *not* do?

"Post anything that could be misinterpreted as an insult or insensitive to others."

Keep It Real

My Pomeranian, Bertie, stumbled into stardom: a succession of videos had already gone semi-viral when, in 2018, he donned a Paddington Bear costume and lit up the internet for a brief moment. The *Paddington Bear* film had just come out, and the uncanny likeness Bert had to the star created some magic: newspapers flew in to take photos, he was on the *Rachael Ray Show* (super random!), and he did a bunch of interviews. My favorite part was when Hugh Bonneville (who plays the dad in the *Paddington* movies) commented on the photo. But the best way to use social media is to share your life—and your pet—with friends and the public. I take photos and videos of Bert during our life together; it is very rare that I ever organize a "shoot."

Kathy's Story

I have never taken social media too seriously, nor become too competitive. Having an Instagram for my dog is, in itself, ridiculous, and the fact that he makes money promoting brands is even more absurd. If you had told me this would happen when I adopted Bert seven years ago, I would have laughed in your face. Yes, it is an unlooked-for boon that companies want to pay Bert to share their products, and I do have to take that seriously, but the only reason he is popular is because I don't take it *too* seriously. Normally, we are happy together living our real life—working at the art gallery, going to the dog park, playing fetch, or swimming in the pool—and, as often as I can, I snatch a quick photo.

@BERTIEBERTTHEPOM
Bertie
Instagram: 444k
Facebook: 20k

Breed
Pomeranian

Human
Kathy Grayson

Favorite Dogs
@157ofgemma
@kokoro_official
@oaksoosoo

@LOUBOUTINANYC
Louboutina
Instagram: 186k

Breed
Golden Retriever

Human
César Fernández-Chavéz

Favorite Dogs
@fortheloveofsmiley
@popeyethefoodie
@the_kardoggians

Spread Love

Petting a dog is known to lower your blood pressure, so imagine the benefits of getting a hug, or a kiss, from that dog! Louboutina helps many people by sharing unconditional affection, and this has led to success on social media. The beautiful thing is that she was not trained to hug. Maybe your dog, too, has a natural, loving skill that the world needs to know about. Louboutina is a good traveler and loves to wear sunglasses—a bit of diva sassiness keeps her followers eager to see what she is up to.

César's Story

I am an introverted person, but Louboutina is very sociable. When she was a puppy, I hugged her a lot; then, when she was about 3 years old, she reciprocated and started hugging me back. In 2016, she featured on Mashable as the most affectionate dog in New York City. The second big viral moment was February 2017, when she was featured in *Time Out* and the *New York Post*, and on *Good Morning America*, the *Rachael Ray Show*, and others. People were already posting pictures of Louboutina on social media, so I decided to create an account for her. She is nicknamed "The Hugging Dog" and we've been involved in many cool projects and TV shows, but what we love most is helping others. We have met people fighting cancer, helped a guy visiting NYC propose to his girlfriend—these are the stories that make Louboutina a symbol of spreading love.

Highlight Your Bond

Our followers have shown us that our most casual posts are our best ones. These include routine family events such as mealtime, the children playing, and, of course, nap time—we all enjoy these magical moments of tranquility. We have worked hard at the bond between our children and Brego and Nami, and we educate the children to be aware of the basic rules of coexistence with dogs (who are always supervised by an adult). This has made it possible for us to enjoy being all together. When people ask us how we achieve this great relationship between our dogs and our children, we always recommend practicing being calm indoors. Brego and Nami are very active dogs, so it is important that they learn to be relaxed inside the house.

@FRAMETHEWEIM
Brego and Nami
Instagram: 121k

Breed
Weimaraner

Human
Marc Calvo Garcia

Favorite Dogs
@harlowandsage
@kopernikk
@thiswildidea

Marc's Story

When people ask me how I decided to create an Instagram account for my dogs, the short answer is that, actually, they stole mine! My personal account became increasingly filled with photos of them, and the reactions to my posts were totally about them. So I changed my username to @frametheweim and dedicated the account to "framing" the life of my Weimaraner. Bit by bit, the account found its purpose and became bigger with the addition of Nami to our family, highlighting her relationship with Brego. The birth of our son added to the equation. And now our great team has grown again with the arrival of our daughter.

Get Travel Ready

From capturing content while on vacation to being invited to visit and promote pet-friendly resorts, some of the most exciting parts of being a dog influencer involve travel. But before you start traveling, it's important to prepare your pup so they're comfortable and ready to take this step. This section focuses mainly on air travel, as it's the most involved type, but most of the information here applies to other forms of travel as well.

▶ The dog carrier

When choosing a carrier, look for one that is large enough for your pup to turn around in easily, but also small enough to fit under an airline seat if your pup is flying in-cabin (remember to check the size restrictions for your particular airline). Beyond that, I recommend carriers with outside pockets for easy access to your dog's essentials (treats, water bowl, toys, poop bags, leash, paperwork, etc.). Once you've selected a carrier, leave it out so your pup can sniff it and get acclimated to it. The goal is for the carrier to feel like your pup's safe place away from home. Creating positive associations with it, like giving them a treat or praise when they go inside, is a great way to do this.

PRO TIP

When flying, be aware that if you have a layover you have to abide by the rules of the layover location as well as your final destination.

Start small

Before the big trip, get your pup used to traveling and being in the carrier for short trips. Test out "traveling" around your neighborhood, so your dog becomes accustomed to staying in the carrier. As they become more comfortable, slowly extend the duration. Anything you can do to get your pup used to traveling before the big trip like taking drives, starting with quick trips and then extending to multi-hour road trips will help. They're going to need to be comfortable staying in the bag for the entire flight, so this step is very important.

Do your research

Check all the rules. Individual airlines have their own policies, ranging from restrictions on dog size, age, and breed, to varying pet fees. Some airlines allow dogs to fly in the cabin, others do not. And generally your dog will be counted as a "carry-on." Different countries also have their own rules. Some just require a health certificate, while others charge fees and require vaccinations, extra paperwork, or even quarantine. Make an appointment with your veterinarian 1–2 months before travel to ensure you have enough time to get any necessary vaccinations. Rabies titer (antibodies) tests, for example, can take weeks to come back. Hotels and car-rental companies have their own rules as well. In summary, when traveling with your pup, make sure to research the policies associated with every aspect of your trip—for your final destination and all stops along the way.

▲ Pack the essentials

Pack everything you might need for the trip—see the checklist for a handy list of things to bring. Favorite toys will feel familiar and comforting for them, and favorite bones will keep them entertained—both on the flight and during the trip. Additionally, depending on the weather and how sensitive your pup is, you might also want to pack a sweater or cooling vest. Since I have a Frenchie, and they're very temperature sensitive, I always pack one or the other depending on the season. Keep everything you'll need for the flight, plus some extras (especially food), in your carry-on, in case your luggage gets lost or delayed. I also pack extra food in general in case my trip gets unexpectedly extended. Better safe than sorry!

CHECKLIST

- ☑ Dog carrier (line with a pee pad in case your pup has an accident or gets sick)
- ☑ Health certificate (plus any additional required paperwork)
- ☑ Food (pack extra)
- ☑ Treats
- ☑ Any medications
- ☑ Favorite toy(s)
- ☑ Favorite bone(s)
- ☑ Leash and harness
- ☑ Water and food bowls
- ☑ Pee pads (pack extra)
- ☑ Poop bags

▲ Go time!

You picked a dog carrier, prepped your pup, did your research, packed the essentials, and now it's time to travel! Your pup will be most comfortable traveling if the airport experience is stress-free, they don't have to go to the bathroom mid-flight, and they aren't full of unspent energy while sitting in their carrier. Plan to leave an hour earlier than you normally would, to give yourself extra time to have your paperwork checked and your pup cleared for travel. And before leaving for the airport, avoid feeding, limit water intake, and take your pup on an extra-long walk so they can burn off excess energy and have ample opportunity to go to the bathroom. While more and more airports are adding pet-relief areas and other pet amenities, not all have these options. Check to see if yours does, and if so how far they are from your gate, so you know what to expect. I walk my pup before leaving for the airport and again when we arrive at the airport. If we can't visit a pet-relief area, I take a pee pad into the restroom to give her one more chance to go to the bathroom before boarding. While on the flight, I give her her favorite bone so she can entertain herself. Once we land, our first stop is the pet-relief area or bathroom.

You're now cleared for takeoff!

@THE_BIKE_DOG
Sox
Instagram: 173k

Breed
Siberian Husky

Human
Michael Fiala

Favorite Dogs
@henrythecoloradodog
@loki
@sar_pup

Go on Adventures

When people make plans to travel, they will often have to find a dog sitter. Try to rearrange your plans to include your dog. Think "What can I do with my dog on this trip?" and seek those opportunities out instead. You probably formed a lot of your life goals before you even got a dog, but when you bring a dog into your life, you make a commitment to include them. Basic obedience training is super important. A well-behaved dog is welcome almost anywhere, and doors open when you are able to trust your dog. People enjoy watching the beautiful adventures we go on and seeing our bond grow, and this naturally creates great content. The most engaging part of an account is its authenticity. Our best-performing content isn't an incredible hike, but personal moments such as the pair of us sleeping.

Michael's Story

I've always dreamed about visiting all 50 states, 62 national parks, and 154 national forests. I felt bad when I traveled and couldn't bring Sox along, so I made it my goal to include him on every trip for the rest of his life. Most people don't follow the desire to travel with total conviction—they come up with reasons to put it off and then regret not doing it. Though my international travel has slowed down, I know I can travel on a motorcycle from state to state easily with Sox. I have found the things we can both do, and know I will enjoy those things more if we are together.

Explore the Outdoors

You know that happy, excited reaction your dog has when you say "walk"? Their tails wag and bodies zigzag as they take in all the new sights, sounds, smells, and (if they're anything like Wiley) tastes—and that kind of happiness is sure to shine through your outdoor photos. You're taking them to explore the world and bringing your followers on the adventure with you. The combination of adorable dogs and stunning scenery is a winning one. So, get out there, explore the world, and take your four-legged friend with you; your dog and your followers will love you all the more for it.

Lexi's Story

I have lived in Colorado my entire life and been blessed with an incredible "backyard" to play in. But it wasn't until Wiley that I started to truly appreciate it. When Wiley was just 10 weeks old, I tucked him into my backpack to blaze the Colorado trails, and we haven't stopped since. From sleeping on the beach in California, to seeing the world from over 14,000ft (4,000m) high in southern Colorado, sprinting down sand dunes, staring up giant redwoods, and leaping into chilly alpine lakes—with so much world and so little time, the adventure never stops. It was never about the likes. It has always been about the smile on Wiley's face; the photos and followers are just a side-effect of that larger mission. His life may be short, but Wiley's world will be wide, and it is a blast bringing people along on that journey.

@HI.WILEY
Wiley

Instagram: 191k
TikTok: 65k

Breed
Dalmatian

Human
Lexi Smith

Favorite Dogs
@dogswiss
@henrythecoloradodog
@thiswildidea

@MJ_THE_BEAGLE
MJ and Will

Instagram: 99k
Facebook: 30k
(@BeagleMJ)

Breed
Beagle

Human
Noam Thiam-Cohen

Favorite Dogs
@lecorgi
@malcolm_the_akita
@narcos_cockerspaniel

Have Fun

If I had a single tip for you when it comes to sharing your dog's daily life on Instagram, it would be: Have fun! Having fun is a great way to strengthen your relationship with your dog and their confidence in you. Your dog will feel good and, trust me, they will give back to you if you decide to take pictures of them. Make your photoshoots a game. Your dog will be at ease and offer you the most beautiful expressions for natural photos that are full of life. And, if you're having fun, so will your community. Being able to convey emotions through your content is the key to success. Have fun and be creative, while letting your dog guide you. Your dog is your first source of inspiration.

Noam's Story
MJ was my very first dog. In the beginning, I didn't know much about dog care, and Instagram turned out to be a great source of information. Sharing MJ's daily dog life was really fun for me, and it seems people also have fun following MJ's, and now MJ and his son Will's, routine. Thanks to their community, I have collaborated with beautiful brands, been invited to fantastic events, and participated in campaigns to raise awareness, or money, for great causes. But, more importantly, I've met some wonderful people—some have become friends and others work relationships.

Find Representation

Now that you've established your brand, learned how to create compelling content, and built an engaged community, brands will be interested in partnering with you. But before you start down the branded partnerships path, it's best to have an expert on your side to protect and advise you, and generally help you succeed.

Find the right representation

Once you've built an engaged following of around 50k+ fans, you'll be ready to bring in the right representation to help you take your account to the next level. Look for representation (for example, a manager or agent) that focuses on what your content focuses on—pets—because they will have the specialized knowledge and relationships to help you succeed. When we're evaluating a potential new client at The Dog Agency, we look for overperforming levels of engagement—not only from a hard-numbers perspective, but also in softer ways, by, for example, taking a deep dive into the comments to determine how invested the audience is. We also look for high-quality and engaging content. Another important part of the evaluation process is getting to know the owner and pet. Do they have a strong bond? Will the owner be reliable and responsive, put effort into their work, and submit their content on time? These are all essential elements in being marketable to brands. When brands are paying you, you need to treat this like your job, because it is.

Protect what you've built

Your representation will advise on whether terms and compensation are favorable and fair to you. They will also help you decide if the usage rights (how, where, and for how long a brand can use your content) and any exclusivity (the limiting of your ability to work with others) granted to a brand partner are appropriate. Bad terms can unreasonably limit your ability to partner with others, and if you're not a lawyer or an industry expert, you may not realize what to look out for—and to avoid—in these types of contracts. Even if you are a lawyer, chances are you're busy and may not have the time or the specialized knowledge to negotiate your dog's contracts. Additionally, when it comes to working with brands, it's best to let your representation be the "bad guy" and push back if a brand asks for too much. They'll also handle any other issues that may pop up along the way, all of which allows you to focus on creating great content.

Leverage your representation's relationships and expertise

Your representation will help get you in front of the right people (brands, press, and so on). Additionally, brands and press outlets generally prefer to work with agencies because it makes their jobs easier and more efficient. Without agencies they'd have to spend a lot of time researching viable dog influencers, sending blind outreach emails and managing communications throughout the campaign with each influencer rather than having one point of contact. Working with an agency like The Dog Agency provides not only ready access to proven influencers, but also strategic campaign guidance and talent management throughout.

PRO TIP

In addition to leveraging their connections, your representation will also give you expert advice to help develop your brand, act as a partner to brainstorm and think through ideas with, and handle a lot of behind-the-scenes work, so you can focus on creating great content.

Go Viral

There is no magic formula for viral videos, even for the most seasoned creator. The basic principle, though, is that you need to create something "unprecedented." That may seem daunting, but think of it on a small scale: even a new joke or skit you thought of can be unprecedented. It could be the way your subject looks or acts, or it could be the information (if it's educational), or even the way it's filmed. The content will always be the most important part, but there are a few things you can do to improve your chances of going viral: Pay attention to when you post your video—timing can be everything; optimize your format for the platform you're posting on; and structure your video to hook the viewer at the beginning. How you go about promoting the video also plays a part.

Ryan's Story

I started a blog and Facebook page for my little dachshund, Crusoe, in 2011. It was just a spur-of-the-moment attempt at a creative outlet, with no goal or intention of making it into what it eventually became. Completely organically, however, it grew and grew, eventually becoming a full-time career for me in 2015. Crusoe is now a *New York Times* best-selling pup with two books, a People's Choice Award for Animal Star, and combined video views of over 1 billion. It's safe to say he changed my life, and I am so happy he did, because my job is now to spend time with my dog.

@CRUSOE_DACHSHUND
Crusoe

Facebook: 3.1m
TikTok: 1.4m
YouTube: 1.3m
Instagram: 820k
Twitter: 33k
(@Celeb_Dachshund)

Breed
Dachshund

Human
Ryan Beauchesne

Favorite Dogs
@harlowandsage
@itsadaphneday
@tunameltsmyheart

@COCOTHEMALTESEDOG
Coco and Cici

TikTok: 2.5m
Instagram: 284k
Facebook: 35k

Breed
Maltese

Human
Jessie Robinson

Favorite Dogs
@fortheloveofsmiley
@mr.biggie
@reagandoodle

Be On Trend

Many big social-media trends occur on platforms run by influencers, so it can be super funny when a dog puts their own spin on it. When coming up with content ideas, my first thought is always "What is trending right now?" We follow trends, but it is also important to stand out from the rest. Find what makes you special and makes you *you*! There are so many animals on social media that it can be hard to be different. Try thinking about how you can take a trend and make it your own. Add props, be relatable, do a trick while incorporating the trend, add a funny caption, be cute—and most of all, have fun. We incorporate all these into our posts and not only do we love it, but others do too.

Jessie's Story

I have had Maltese my entire life, and when I was 17 Coco and her sister Cici became my family's newest additions. I started the account on day one and it took off. I never planned on having "social-media famous" dogs, but I continued to post pictures every day and people adored them. Coco eventually started doing "paws up" and this created her brand. Having their pictures taken is everything for the girls, as they love to impress me and get treats. Whenever it's time to take pictures, they wag their tails with excitement. Coco and Cici make so many people around the world happy just by being who they are.

Leverage Connections

The more time I spend around animals, the more I realize we have way more to learn from them than they from us. The most popular quotation I hear about leveraging connections is, "It's not what you know, it's who you know." There's truth to this, but I find it unfulfilling, too self-centered. The animal kingdom gives us a better understanding. The powerful Belgian draft horse can pull 8,000lbs (3,600kg) on its own. If you harness up two that have never worked together, they will easily pull 20,000lbs (9,000kg). But here is where the magic happens: two that grew up together, trained together, and have a solid working relationship will pull up to 30,000lbs (13,600kg). This is a perfect example of synergy, of leveraging connections.

Noah's Story

Since Milo and I joined The Dog Agency (TDA), I've seen synergy like this in action. My background is in marketing and public relations, so I wasn't sure I would benefit from representation. I could pull 8,000lbs on my own, but now TDA and I are pulling well over 30,000lbs. TDA knows my goals and has helped me build an account that balances animal content, mental-health awareness, social justice, humor, fitness, and more. I've had partnerships I never would've dreamed of, smoothly executed and beneficial for everyone involved. I trust TDA to propel me forward and protect me from harmful contracts or unsuitable partnerships. Their representation has reduced the stress of navigating a complex industry, allowing me to focus on being the best dog dad to Milo.

@MILOANDNOAH
Milo

TikTok: 399k
Instagram: 69k

Breed
Mini Goldendoodle

Human
Noah Haislah

Favorite Dogs
@agoldennamedkevin
@itslolathehusky
@loki

Brand Partnerships

You are now ready to work with brands.
To be successful here, you need to understand
what brands look for when selecting influencers
to market their products, and also what to look
out for when deciding whether or not to partner
with a given brand.

Be marketable

As an influencer, your value is literally your ability
to influence people. If your audience cares about
what you're saying, brands will care about you.
One of the main ways brands gauge how engaged
your audience is is by calculating your engagement
rate. Engagement rate is typically calculated by
dividing the number of interactions with your content
by your total following. The higher this number, the
better. Brands also care about your ability to influence
purchase decisions, the size of your audience, the
quality of your content, and the type of content you
create (for example, are you an authentic fit
to represent them?).

The Golden Rule:
Keep it authentic

Who you choose to work with, and how often you
choose to post sponsored content, will reflect on your
brand, which is your most valuable asset. So, make these
decisions wisely. Just as brands research influencers to
determine whether they want to work with them, you
should also do your research and only agree to work with
partners that align with your content and values. Do you
like the potential partner's products? Do you believe in
their mission? Are there any concerning issues with them
that could reflect poorly on you for choosing to partner
with them? Also, keep in mind what drew people to
follow you in the first place—your organic content. They
didn't follow you to get a stream of ads, so make sure to
space out your promotional posts or you'll risk turning
off your audience and losing credibility. Maintaining
trust and interest with your community is of the utmost
importance. The most successful influencers are guided
by authenticity not dollar signs. While getting paid offers
is exciting, remember how hard you had to work to get
to this point and how much work you put into building a
community that trusts you. You don't want to risk losing it
all for a quick payday that alienates your audience.

Understand what the partnership entails

After determining if the brand is an authentic fit, you need to understand what is being asked of you before you move forward and enter into a legally binding contract. What kind of content are you being asked to create? What guidelines are associated with that content? Is there any exclusivity involved? If so, how broad is the exclusivity: does it cover all of the brand's competitors, or is it just tied to a specific category, such as treats? How long is the exclusive period? You might be open to one month of exclusivity, but what if they are looking for a year? What usage rights will the brand have with your content and your name and likeness? And how long will those rights last? That last part is very important because if a brand is using your likeness to promote their products, their competitors might not be interested in working with you, and you could lose out on potential future opportunities. Lastly, is the payment offered fair for what is being asked of you? Good representation will navigate all of this with you, helping you understand the terms and advise if the partnership is right for you.

Show up for the brand

Hooray! You've determined that the brand is an authentic fit, you understand what the partnership entails, and it is in line with your expectations. You are ready to proceed with the partnership. Now, you need to show up for the brand. First, read through all the creative guidelines carefully (to find out all the dos and don'ts) and take note of the deadlines—both content delivery deadlines and posting dates. Next, it's time to get creative. The best branded content feels natural on your page, while also meeting the brand's goals. So, stay true to the guidelines and create engaging content that incorporates the brand in an authentic way. Content that makes people want to share it—either by tagging a friend or sending it to them—will perform best in terms of engagement and awareness. If you follow the guidelines, meet the deadlines, and deliver high-performing content, the brand will be inclined to work with you again.

Note: If your brand partnership involves shooting on location, make sure to check out Road to Fame: Life On Set, page 102.

@LILYBUG_LPB
Bug
TikTok: 147k
Instagram: 98k

Breed
American Staffordshire Terrier

Human
Marisa Grimshaw

Favorite Dogs
@157ofgemma
@noah_and_lincoln
@tikatheiggy

Maintain Your Brand

Having a consistent and authentic voice is key for any social account because it allows your followers to trust you and form a personal connection to you. Staying true to yourself is just as important when it comes to brand partnerships. Your followers can tell when something feels off-brand, and will be less likely to engage or to trust what you share or suggest in future. Whether you're working with an agency, fielding inbounds from interested brands, or reaching out to brands, always ask: Does this campaign feel authentic to me and my account? Would I use the product regardless of payment or product exchange? Can I maintain an authentic voice in the captions/copy of this campaign? Am I providing added value to my followers by sharing it?

Marisa's Story

Having started Bug's Instagram many years ago, and before brands were interested in working with us, I spent a lot of time sharing very honest posts and stories with our followers. This included everything from our strong bond and Bug's love of hugging, to the basic training we work on daily, to our struggles with her allergies and the trusted products I have painstakingly researched. While I would never pretend to have the knowledge of a veterinarian or professional trainer, our page did become a trusted resource for others seeking advice. With that in mind, it's become incredibly easy for me to identify the brands I want to work with and the campaigns I'm eager to accept.

Find the Best Lighting

Dog photography can be challenging. You don't need to be a professional, however, to be a great photographer. I mostly use an iPhone, but the detail of Charlie's black fur tends to be lost, which can make creating good-quality content challenging. There are some easy tips and tricks that have helped me. First, make sure you have proper lighting: inside, I opt for lots of natural light; outside, I try to avoid direct sunlight as it creates glare on some parts of Charlie's coat and shadows on others. Also, choose a backdrop that creates a nice contrast to your dog's fur and doesn't distract from your subject—for example, brighter, blurred, or less busy. Finally, remember that practice makes perfect: trial and error is important. Try different backdrops and lighting and find what works best for you.

Camilla's Story

I originally started Charlie's Instagram account to keep track of the great memories we build together. Never did I think that he would gain so much popularity so quickly! His unique look and goofy personality continue to capture hearts. Charlie has always been a natural in front of the camera—even as a small puppy he would look straight into the lens and hold his pose for me. I capture Charlie doing the things he loves most: hiking, training, playing with friends ... and just being his silly self. I always turn creating content into a fun learning opportunity; that mental stimulation goes a long way for a working breed like Charlie, and his enthusiasm shines straight through!

@CHARLIE_THEBLACKSHEPHERD
Charlie

TikTok: 311k
Instagram: 273k

Breed
German Shepherd

Human
Camilla Cools

Favorite Dogs
@dognamedstella
@enzo.swe
@kelly_bove

Life On Set

When moving from creating content on your own with your pup, to working on set with a crew, there are some additional things to keep in mind.

Understand expectations and set guidelines

First make sure that the planned shoot is within your and your pup's comfort zone before you agree to participate. Know what is expected of your dog, and set guidelines in advance so things run smoothly and there are no surprises for you, your dog, or the on-set team. Also find out how long the shoot is expected to take and make sure that ample breaks have been scheduled for your pup to go to the bathroom, drink water, and rest.

Be prepared and pay attention

Pack everything you'll need for the day (treats, water bowl, leash, pee mat, bone for breaks etc.) and arrange to get to the set early, so your dog can sniff around, meet the crew, and feel relaxed by the time you're ready to start. The set is likely a new environment for your pup, so pay extra attention to their behavioral cues and take things slowly—if they look stressed, ask for a quick break. Stay on set, or have someone both you and your dog trust on set with your pup at all times, for their comfort and your peace of mind. Lastly, remember to reward your pup with treats for their hard work throughout the day!

PRO TIP

Crews are often focused on getting the best shot, and rightly so, but they may not be used to working with dogs. If they suggest something that will make you or your dog uncomfortable—like setting your dog up somewhere high—speak up and politely suggest alternative ideas.

▲ Capture behind-the-scenes (#BTS) content

In addition to being a job, this should also be fun for you and your pup. Remember to take behind-the-scenes photos and videos to capture this exciting experience. This is something I often forget to do because I get caught up in the moment, and always regret it. Before posting or publicly sharing any #bts content, first check with the production crew to make sure it's OK—they might have restrictions on what can be shared and when.

Watch out for toxins

Lastly, as with any new environment, make sure there's nothing harmful your dog can get into. Sets often have snacks out for the cast and crew, but they may not be pup-friendly. There may be chocolate around (the darker it is, the more toxic to pups), and grapes (or raisins hidden in cookies for example), and all sorts of things containing xylitol (artificial sweetener). Watching out for the first two is easy, but the third can sneak up on you in surprising places, including in peanut butter, which is frequently used as a treat. Always check labels.

@DUCKYTHEYORKIE
Ducky

TikTok: 1.9m
Instagram: 74k

Breed
Yorkshire Terrier

Human
Christine Hsu

Favorite Dogs
@frankie.the.sausage
@orkyeh
@pebblestheceo

Have a Consistent Aesthetic

Developing a consistent visual style for your pup is a very important part of having a successful account. I want Ducky's fans to know what to expect when they browse his content, so I strive to keep a consistent aesthetic no matter the medium or platform. Whether it's the setting, the accessories, the editing, or the colors, I try to make sure there is always a common thread that ties all the posts together. This does not mean you shouldn't try to evolve or improve this style, but identifying what is working and sticking to it consistently will go a long way toward highlighting your pup's account.

Christine's Story

I started fashion blogging in 2012, and after I got Ducky in 2013 I knew I had to share his cuteness with the world. He was the most adorable pup I had ever seen, but it was difficult to imagine running multiple accounts at the time. Four years later, I decided I was finally ready, and that's when I began heavily focusing on Ducky's accounts. I applied the things I learned from my own experience to help grow Ducky's pages, and I have been so happy to know that everyone shares my love for him! When I receive messages from his fans about how Ducky helps them throughout their day, it seriously makes our day and helps motivate us to continue producing content that we both love.

Find a BFF

There are many benefits to having two well-matched dogs: they can become BFFs, providing each other with companionship and a built-in playmate. Taking care to select the right dog can ensure that they get along well and develop a good bond. If your current dog is more of a couch potato, bringing in a high-energy breed could be annoying to them. Instead, choose a dog whose energy level and temperament are similar. As Lizzie and Ally are golden retrievers they are naturally very chill, and this makes it easier to take photos of them together. I try to showcase their bond by capturing precious moments as and when they happen. Sometimes, I ask the girls to pose for me and they always get rewarded with lots of treats!

Fran's Story

I wasn't certain I wanted to add a second dog to our family. We had adopted Lizzie a year earlier when the opportunity came up to get a puppy. I never realized how much more fun it would be to have two dogs until we brought Ally home and the bond between them really developed. They've become sisters and best friends, initiating play every day, whether it's a game of chase or some wrestling. When I see these playful moments, or their cuddles, it fills my heart with so much joy that I know we made the right choice.

@LIZZIE.BEAR
Lizzie and Ally
Instagram: 429k

Breed
Golden Retriever

Human
Fran Laurendeau

Favorite Dogs
@george_and_troja
@henrythecoloradodog
@nemoccr

Expand Revenue Streams

Opportunities for dog influencers started with digital branded campaigns, but, as the industry grew, the demand for dog influencers expanded beyond social media. From appearing in movies and music videos, to getting book deals, the opportunities these days are endless. Launching merchandise is a great way to start expanding beyond branded campaigns.

◄ Print-on-demand merchandise

A great entry point is print-on-demand merchandise. You can set up your own online store (on Shopify, for example) for a minimal fee to feature your products, which is great for branding purposes. If, however, you want no upfront costs, you can link directly to a print-on-demand website. Print-on-demand companies handle both production and fulfillment, and have tons of merchandise options to select from, including T-shirts, hats, bathing suits, calendars, and even engraved jewelry. They're an easy and cost-effective way to offer a variety of different products. When designing merchandise, get creative! Think about what excites your audience, and maybe even invite them to participate in the process, by, for example, letting them vote on potential designs, so they feel involved and connected to the final product.

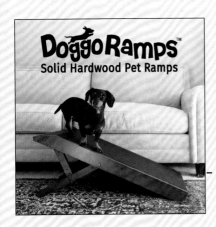

▲ Manufacture your own products

Once you've established demand for your products through print-on-demand, you will be armed with insight as to whether manufacturing your own products makes sense for you. It would allow you to create unique products—like DoggoRamps by Crusoe (page 90)—and could come with a higher return, but it involves more risk and more work. If you do choose to create your own products, there are companies that can make the process easier for you and reduce the risk. Crowdfunding platforms (such as Kickstarter and Indiegogo) lower the risk tied to production by helping you raise the funds needed to manufacture your products. Once you have manufactured your products, fulfillment companies (such as ShipMonk) lower the work involved by handling the packing, shipping, and returns management of your orders.

Licensing

Licensing is another path you can take that, similar to print-on-demand, removes risk and reduces your workload. With licensing, the company you license to will handle production and use their relationships to distribute your products in retail outlets. In exchange, you'll be paid a royalty, an upfront fee, or a combination of the two. However, when entering into licensing agreements, make sure you understand what rights you are granting, how those rights can be used, for how long, and what approvals you have over the final products. It is best to have an expert review the agreement before you enter into it, to make sure the terms meet your expectations.

Set Up Shop

An online shop allows you to connect with an audience in a new way. Establishing a shop is quite easy; the hard part is taking your dog-owner hat off and imagining yourself as a buyer. The key is knowing your audience and appealing to their needs. Product selection is vital to success. Of course, I have made mistakes (which I've learned from), but I am lucky enough to have a huge global platform via Puggy Smalls's social network, and I am able to study analytics of sales and posts to gain a clear understanding of what people and their pets want.

@THEPUGGYSMALLS
Puggy Smalls
TikTok: 468k
Facebook: 236k
Instagram: 194k

Breed
Pug

Human
Nick Ettridge

Favorite Dogs
@izzythe.frenchie
@mr.biggie
@pop_sausage

Nick's Story

I initially used social media to proudly archive memories of my boy to share with friends. One video of Puggy in a desk drawer, titled *Pug in a Drawer* and captioned "How to sneak your dog into work," went viral overnight, with millions of views, and I instantly saw how much joy Puggy brings to others. My obsession with creating content of my dog quickly turned into a brand and a business, allowing me to spend every minute of every day with my beloved boy. The shop started with a sticker. This quickly turned into calendars, T-shirts, and a range of cards. To keep Puggy super relatable, I sourced dog versions of the latest brands seen on human celebs and influencers—The Dog Face and Pucci, among others. Now I have a platform for awesome Puggy content, personal video messages, and merch to gear up your dog.

@GONETOTHESNOWDOGS
Memphis and Kira

Facebook: 2.7m
YouTube: 1m
TikTok: 717k
Instagram: 246k
Twitter: 19k
(@Gone2theSnowDog)

Breed
Siberian Husky

Humans
Jessica and Jamie Hatch

Favorite Dogs
@crusoe_dachshund
@loki
@thesupercollies

Diversify Your Platforms

Diversifying platforms is extremely important! YouTube, Instagram, Facebook, TikTok—all these platforms need to be treated in different ways, and all have massive potential for you and your brand. Jumping on all of them at once can be difficult, but, over time, as you perfect your craft, trying out new social-media platforms is always a great idea. Not every platform will work for every creator, so play around with them and have some fun. You can take content you have already produced and restructure it for a new platform.

Jessica and Jamie's Story

We have jumped on just about every new platform there is. Some of them have been successful and others not so much, but we always try to have fun with it. By posting across multiple platforms, our reach on all of them has grown. We have found success not only in reaching new audiences that might otherwise never have discovered us, but also in rediscovering followers who used to watch our content on different platforms! We have also found that diversifying platforms really helps with our creativity, since no two platforms are the same. We learn to create in different ways.

Don't Overthink It

Rocco has taught me not to take life so seriously! He is just a dog who loves life and is always smiling. I keep my phone on me at all times in case he does something weird or silly. People love his videos, because he has a happy-go-lucky personality and he doesn't care what anyone thinks—and people can relate to that. I focus on the clumsy and goofy personality traits that do best on his channel. Some of it is accidental: most of his viral posts were of Rocco being Rocco, and were not staged. Keep your camera phone or camera handy, and play up your pet's personality and the quirks that make them unique.

Erin's Story

I had no intention of Rocco becoming a social-media star. I needed a place to put all the pictures and videos I was taking of him, so I made him his own Instagram. He's a naturally clumsy dog so I wanted to make sure his account highlighted his goofy personality. His most well-known video is of his floofy butt as he tried to climb into a chair. The video is low quality and I just happened to have my phone on hand to capture this real-life moment. The video is relatable (the struggle is real!) and made people smile. If you search for "clumsiest dog on the internet" or "clumsiest dog in the world," Rocco will pop up!

@ROCCO_RONI
Rocco

TikTok: 2.5m
(@rocco_)
Instagram: 113k
Facebook: 52k
(@RoccoAndWhiskey)

Breed
Old English Sheepdog

Human
Erin Einbender

Favorite Dogs
@dunkinandfriends
@joshthedoodle
@mayapolarbear

@DOGNAMEDSTELLA

Stella and Mabel

Instagram: 407k
Facebook: 265k
YouTube: 56k

Breed
Labrador Retriever

Human
Jody Hartman

Favorite Dogs
@fredtheafghan
@h2oboys
@labradicious

Film Everything

In order to capture those hilarious and overly dramatic moments in a dog's life, the camera always has to be rolling. Having plenty of footage to work with allows you to edit clips down to only the most entertaining shots and create fast-moving, compilation-style videos that appeal to the attention spans of today. Even the most basic of dog behavior can be exaggerated through interesting camera angles, music or sound effects, and editing. Keep the thinking simple and film all those funny everyday behaviors and nuances, then blow them way out of proportion and have fun with it.

Jody's Story

I used to document Stella's quirky behavior in short, comedic videos that I'd post sporadically on my personal social-media accounts; then, one day, I put one on YouTube. The video *Stella's Dog Brakes* illustrated a strangely funny behavior involving Stella dropping her hind legs while running. Within two days, it was viewed over 7 million times and became the #1 most popular YouTube video in the world. I began filming Stella more and more, following the formula that made the dog-brakes video such a hit: different shots of a behavior, humorously edited together with a few basic jump cuts. Getting videos to regularly trend without much of an audience proved challenging, so I created an Instagram account for Stella, filmed everything, edited non-stop, and posted very regularly in order to build an online audience.

Keep a Posting Cadence

With an account name like @dailydougie, we set expectations early on, but posting daily wasn't hard for us—like any new puppy owner, we were confident ours was the cutest! We both work full-time, so we generally post first thing in the morning. This provides the structure we need, and our followers know when to expect a post. The hard part is coming up with creative and interesting photos every day! We benefit from of a couple of "built-in" content days: for example, many dog accounts post a tongue-out photo on Tuesdays, using the hashtag #tongueouttuesday. We have also created our own "built-in" content: on Fridays we post videos of Dougie being petted or brushed, or snoring, with the hashtag #fridaymomentofzen. Find something interesting your pet does and create your own weekly hashtag.

Anita's Story

Our approach has mostly been to focus on what Dougie does best: look cute anywhere and everywhere. He's not very well trained, but he's sweet, gentle, and pretty lazy. We don't usually have a problem getting his attention, but the occasional treat incentive doesn't hurt. He is our family dog and we are just documenting him doing regular family-dog things. We weren't trying to become popular on Instagram when we started the account in 2014, and we have made an effort to keep it low-key and not ask too much of Dougie. We feel like we've struck the right balance, allowing our followers to witness Dougie's well-loved (and well-groomed) life.

@DAILYDOUGIE
Dougie

Instagram: 519k
Facebook: 96k

Breed
Shih Tzu

Human
Anita Rotenberg

Favorite Dogs
@kokistateofmind
@lifewithleroy
@owenthegriff

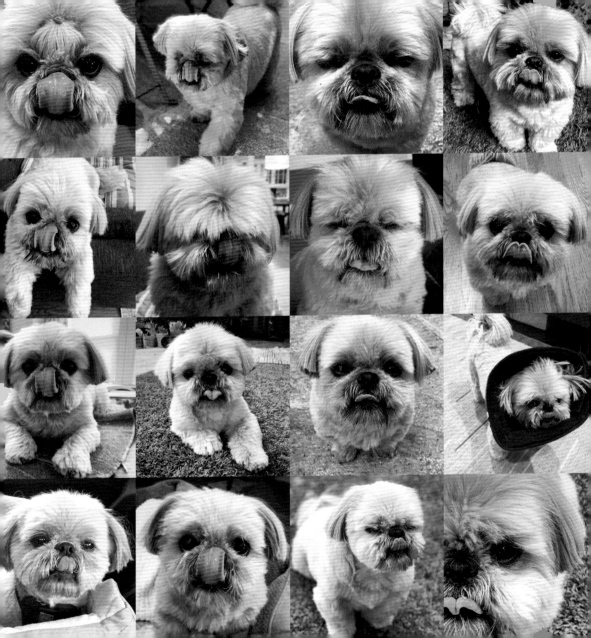

Use Your Influence for Good

Dog influencers spread so much happiness around the world with their content, but one of my favorite things about them is their commitment to using their influence for good. Whether donating profits from their merchandise to causes that are important to them, working with shelters to help pets find their forever homes, or raising awareness about misunderstood breeds, dog influencers have the potential to do so much good in the world.

Choose a cause

Select a cause that is important to you, and then find a nonprofit organization to partner with. Before selecting an organization, do your research. Check their reputation, and understand how they use the money they raise. Smaller organizations are generally more responsive and more in need of help, so don't overlook them!

Get involved

Once you've selected an organization to partner with, be proactive—reach out and ask where they need help. Maybe they have a message they're trying to raise awareness about and you can help by sharing it on your account, or maybe they have a fundraiser going on and you can help them raise money by directing people to it.

PRO TIP

As you embark on this journey, think of ways you can use your influence to have a positive impact. The audience you've built gives you a platform to amplify your voice. Invite your community to join you in doing good and supporting causes that are important to you, and you'll be able to increase your positive impact on the world exponentially.

Invite your community to join you

Let your community know why your cause is important to you, and find ways to invite them to make a difference with you. For example, every year for Chlo's birthday we'd host a charity bash. They were a ton of fun, but, more importantly, we were able to raise both awareness and funds for causes we cared about. Another way you can invite your community to get involved is by selling merchandise you create for the benefit of your cause. If you're artistic, you can create engaging and informative graphics for your community to share to spread awareness. Find a creative way that makes sense for you.

Keep it fresh

Post about your cause regularly, while keeping the content fresh and interesting so your audience stays engaged. If there is an interesting development or update related to your cause, share it. If you reach a fundraising goal or milestone let your audience know. If you created merchandise for the benefit of your cause, let your community know how much you collectively raised. They'll be excited to know the impact you're having together.

@BULLY.BALOO
Baloo

TikTok: 590k
Instagram: 177k

Breed
American Staffordshire Terrier Mix

Human
Isabella Boone

Favorite Dogs
@piratepitbull
@theasherhouse
@the_blueboys

Challenge Stereotypes

Having a message is a huge part of being an influencer. Think about what you want to accomplish with your presence. You can, for example, challenge stereotypes head-on: The media portrays pitbull breeds as scary guard dogs, so post pictures of your pittie in pajamas. Small dogs are thought to be impossible to train, so post videos of your Pomeranian doing incredible tricks. While respecting other people's views and opinions, ask questions that spark conversation. Your posts have the power to affect people's views, and if your content is thought-provoking, you will inspire others and provoke change.

Isabella's Story

As a kid, I always voiced my opinions. It was, therefore, only fitting that I became an advocate for a breed that didn't have a voice of its own after falling in love with my rescue pit bull, or "bully," Baloo. Though I originally started his Instagram for fun, I quickly shifted toward advocacy after realizing how challenging it was to own a breed that was shunned by the general public. Gaining a following wasn't my main goal, but it did help me accomplish some of my other ones: I wanted bully breeds to be included in more pet-related campaigns; I wanted to challenge breed-specific laws; and, more than anything, I wanted people to see pit bulls as pets, not monsters. Baloo has since become one of the most popular faces in bully-breed advocacy, and my goals to challenge the stereotypes of his breed have grown even bigger.

Have a Mission

Think about what is important to you. Posting cute and interesting photos with witty captions is important for a successful account, but it doesn't set you apart. Having a mission for your account will elevate your account and give it more purpose and direction. It's easy to get overwhelmed when trying to figure out a mission, but it doesn't have to be stressful. You can make anything your mission! It can be as big and broad or as small and specific as you want it to be. Your mission can evolve over time—people change and grow and so does the world, so don't feel you have to stick with a mission that is no longer aligned with your values or beliefs.

Joey and Michael's Story

I've always been a fierce animal advocate. I first met Mervin when I worked in a shelter. He was small, fragile, and cranky, so I brought him home as a foster for some extra TLC. Pretty much immediately we knew that he would be staying. Michael and I already had three other rescue dogs and a rescue cat, so we weren't planning on adopting, but we couldn't say goodbye to him. Soon after adoption, he started to get a big following on social media—adopting pets has always been a huge part of our lives, so we knew we would make that our mission. When you adopt you don't only save one life, but two! By adopting, or fostering, you free up critical resources, like kennel space, for the shelter to help another animal.

@MERVINTHECHIHUAHUA
Mervin

Facebook: 287k
Instagram: 124k

Breed
Rescue Chihuahua

Humans
Joey Teixeira
and Michael Keeney

Favorite Dogs
@157ofgemma
@pinkpigletpuppy
@thelilgremlins

BLACK
LIVES
MATTER

@SUPER_SCOOTY
Scooty
Instagram: 140k

Breed
Rescue Mixed Breed

Human
Erica Loring

Favorite Dogs
@desertbunnyandwolf
@jackhecan
@pigeonpup

Share Your Journey

Don't be afraid to make your page a little personal. People are looking for authenticity and will invest in your lives, crying with you on your bad days, and laughing with you when your pet performs silly antics. Many rescue pets have a hard life before they land in their forever home, and it's important to honor that, and remind people that there are brighter days ahead. Pets have an amazing ability to heal, forgive, and forget, and we, as humans, can learn a lot from them. Scooty suffered a great deal before I found her, but you would never know that from her smiling pictures. I make sure to remind people of her original situation and use it to encourage them to consider adopting the dogs who need it most.

Erica's Story

In 2012, Scooty, a 6-month-old stray in Mexico, was hit by a car and left for dead. She was found by Baja Dog Rescue, along with about 100 other dogs, in very rough shape, sick and badly injured. Baja Dog Rescue took in as many dogs as they could and posted a plea for help. I saw pictures of the beautiful, doe-eyed, broken puppy and knew I needed her. It wasn't easy at first; there were a lot of ups and downs and medical expenses. We rehabilitated her with lots of love, patience, and humor. She mastered her wheelchair and the ability to weeble-wobble about. Now, she is known for being the happiest dog with the biggest smile you will ever see!

Champion Courage

We want to show everyone that life with a disabled dog can be good. Mateo is so fun-loving, even with a missing paw. We invested a lot of time and love so that he accepts his prosthesis and can enjoy our long hikes. Of course you must expect more costs than from a healthy dog: veterinarian appointments, X-rays, and a prosthesis that must be changed regularly. But adopting a disabled dog was never a bad decision. If you have experience, give a new life to a dog that others might not want! When we got Mateo we already had a great community that followed our stories. I don't think we grew just because of him, but because our little pack lives together in such an extraordinary way. There is nothing better than to see them happy, but with Mateo it is something else. It gives me joy when he walks around smiling, making the best of his life.

Vanessa's Story

We started as most did. When we got Mojo, our miniature pinscher, we wanted to capture a digital diary on Instagram. My boyfriend became increasingly fond of photography, so he got a camera, and as our photos became more professional, we started to share our lives. Today we are part of a mega community, and we love to share our experience and knowledge, but we get back at least as much as we give! I want to show everyone that Mateo has as much strength and will as our other dogs. He can support people whose dogs need an amputation, but he can just as well give courage to disabled people! Social media has changed my life. The exchange with the community is gold, and nice messages sweeten every day. Through Instagram we have made close friends that we would never have met otherwise.

@VERPINSCHT
Mateo, Mojo, and Rana
Instagram: 95k

Breeds
Miniature Pinscher,
Rescue Mixed Breed

Human
Vanessa Magalhaes

Favorite Dogs
@hergiantlove
@lucathesheltie
@thegoodmutt

@CHLOETHEMINIFRENCHIE
Emma (and Chlo)
Instagram: 161k
Facebook: 60k

Breed
French Bulldog

Human
Loni Edwards

Favorite Dogs
All the dogs!

Leave a Legacy

Choose a cause that's important to you, share why it's important to you, and make it easy for your community to join you in making a difference. When Chlo was killed, I was shocked to discover that under US law dogs are seen as mere property—like a table or chair. As a result, they lack fundamental legal protections. These laws are out of touch with how we view our pets, and I felt the duty to raise awareness about this and push for change. I partnered with the Animal Legal Defense Fund (ALDF) to create a petition (www.aldf.org/animalsnotproperty) that quickly received over 18,000 signatures. Building on that, I created a fundraising page that raised over $20,000 to support the ALDF's mission of advancing animals' interests through the legal system.

Loni's Story

Chlo entered my life in 2013 and my world was forever changed. She was my first pup, first "child," best friend—and business partner. She quickly became one of the first pet influencers, and led to the creation of the first talent management agency for pet influencers, The Dog Agency (@thedogagency), as well as PetCon (@petconofficial). Chlo's life was tragically cut short at just 4 years, but during that time we were able to do a lot of good together, from producing fun charity bashes for her birthdays to partnering with brands on limited-edition charitable products. After losing Chlo, I got Emma Bear to help fill the void in my heart and to carry on Chlo's mission of using influence for good in her honor. Chloe's legacy will live on forever.

Index

Page numbers in *italics* indicate dog pictures.

Picture Glossary

Key: t: top; b: below; l: left; r: right

Learn How to Speak Dog
Page 8: @harlowandsage
Page 9t: @kelly_bove

Road to Fame
Page 16t: @mr.biggie
Page 16b: @tunameltsmyheart
Page 17l: @157ofgemma
Page 17r: @remixthedog
Page 24t: @rocco_roni
Page 24b: @chloetheminifrenchie
Page 25: @tikatheiggy
Page 36t: @brussels.sprout
Page 36b: @chloetheminifrenchie
Page 44t: @remixthedog
Page 44b: @chloetheminifrenchie
Page 45t: @amazinggraciedoodle
Page 45r: @harlowandsage
Page 46: @duckytheyorkie
Page 47: @crusoe_dachshund
Page 58t: @cocothemaltesedog
Page 58b: @super_scooty
Page 59: @popeyethefoodie
Page 60l: @brussels.sprout
Page 60r: @chloetheminifrenchie
Page 61: @louboutinanyc
Page 70: @chloetheminifrenchie
Page 71: @kerith_the_golden_
retriever, Heidi Carman
Page 78t: @duckytheyorkie
Page 78b: @chloetheminifrenchie
Page 80: @popeyethefoodie
Page 81: @chloetheminifrenchie
Page 88: @rileybeann

Page 96: @reagandoodle
Page 97: @chloetheminifrenchie
Page 102: @chloetheminifrenchie
Page 103: @thatgoldendoodle
Page 108t: @mr.biggie
Page 108b: @tikatheiggy
Page 109: @crusoe_dachshund
Page 120: @mervinthechihuahua
Page 121: @chloetheminifrenchie

Credits

Key: t: top; b: below; l: left; r: right

Pages 8, 45, 52–3: Brittni and Jeffrey Vega
Pages 9t, 42–3: Kelly Bove
Page 9b: Inna Astakhova/ Shutterstock
Pages 14–15: Ellée Gudge, Tom Bowman
Pages 16t, 64–5, 108t: Mr. Biggie
Pages 16b, 20–1: @tunameltsmyheart
Pages 17l, 66–7: Gemma Gené @157ofgemma
Pages 17r, 22–3, 44t: Chris Ha – owner of @RemixTheDog
Pages 18–19: Allison Cannarsa-Barr
Pages 24t, 114–15: Photos: @Erin. Loves.Dogs
Pages 25, 30–1, 108b: Thomas Shapiro
Pages 26–7, 59, 80: Ivy Diep
Pages 28–9: Charles Lever
Pages 32–3: @cookiemalibu
Pages 34–5, 103: Macie + Mindy
Pages 36t, 38–9, 60l: @brussels.sprout
Pages 40–1: Josephine Zosa
Pages 45, 50–1: J. Fanny Karpman
Pages 46, 78, 104–105: Christine Hsu, Jason Lu

Pages 47, 90–1, 109: Crusoe the Dachshund
Pages 48–9: Instagram and YouTube: @mayapolarbear
Pages 54–5, 96: Sandi Swiridoff/@ Reagandoodle
Pages 56–7: @BarkleySirCharles on Instagram/Owners: Paul and Melissa C.
Pages 58t, 92–3: Jessie Robinson/ Katee Lauchner
Pages 58b, 126–7: @super_scooty
Page 61, 88: PetCon
Pages 62–3: Sydnee and Ryan Gilletti
Pages 68–9: Steve Greig
Page 71: @kerith_the_golden_ retriever, Heidi Carman
Pages 72–73: Photos: Kathy Grayson
Pages 74–75: César E. Fernández-Chávéz
Pages 76–7: @frametheweim
Pages 82–3: @the_bike_dog
Pages 84–5: Alexis Smith
Pages 86–7: Noam Thiam-Cohen (@Noamtc)
Pages 94–5: Noah Brennan Haislah
Pages 98–9: Marisa Grimshaw
Pages 100–101: Instagram: @charlie_theblackshepherd
Pages 106–107: Fran Laurendeau
Pages 110–11: Puggy Smalls
Pages 112–13: Gone to the Snow Dogs
Pages 116–17: Jody Hartman/ @dognamedstella
Pages 118–19: Anita L. Rotenberg
Pages 120, 124–5: Michael Keeney
Pages 122–3: Instagram: @bully.baloo
Pages 128–9: Rafael Andrade

Acknowledgments

Thank you:

To all the amazing pups and their humans
who shared their stories.

To my first fur baby, Chlo, who introduced
me to the incredible world of pet influencers.

To Emma Bear, the sweetest, cuddliest nugget
who sat in my lap while I wrote this book.

To my endlessly supportive partner
(and the best dog dad!), Steve.

To Dr. Lisa Lippman, who has taught me so
much about pet health and safety over the years.

To Sigrid, editor extraordinaire.

To my hardworking team at The Dog Agency:
Steph, Carly, Rachelle, Allison, and Erin.

And, last but not least, to Andrew, Jodi, and
the wonderful team at Laurence King Publishing
who brought this vision to life!

About the Author

Loni Edwards is a lawyer turned entrepreneur who stumbled
into the incredible world of pet influencers via her late fur baby
Chlo (@chloetheminifrenchie). She is the Founder and CEO of
The Dog Agency (@thedogagency): "The first—and really, only
major—management company for social-media celebrity animal
clients" (*Vogue*). She is also the Founder and CEO of PetCon (@
petconofficial): "The event that brings together the world's most
influential and social-savvy pets" (*Good Morning America*).
She is a graduate of Harvard Law School, Cornell University,
and Phillips Academy Andover, and a director on the board of the
Animal Cancer Foundation. She can be found online at @lonidee.

First published in Great Britain in 2021 by Laurence King,
an imprint of The Orion Publishing Group Ltd.,
Carmelite House, 50 Victoria Embankment,
London EC4Y 0DZ

An Hachette UK Company

10 9 8 7 6 5 4 3 2

A CIP catalogue record for this book is
available from the British Library.

ISBN 978 1 91394 714 9

Origination by DL Imaging, UK
Printed in China by C&C Offset Printing Co. Ltd

Commissioning editor: Andrew Roff
Designer: Florian Michelet

www.laurenceking.com
www.orionbooks.co.uk

Page 98: The BARK and SUPER CHEWER marks and logos
are trademarks of Barkbox, Inc.

Please note: Follower numbers and other statistics
were correct at the original date of publication
but are subject to change.